Ballad of the Buried Life

UNC | COLLEGE OF ARTS AND SCIENCES
Germanic and Slavic Languages and Literatures

From 1949 to 2004, UNC Press and the UNC Department of Germanic & Slavic Languages and Literatures published the UNC Studies in the Germanic Languages and Literatures series. Monographs, anthologies, and critical editions in the series covered an array of topics including medieval and modern literature, theater, linguistics, philology, onomastics, and the history of ideas. Through the generous support of the National Endowment for the Humanities and the Andrew W. Mellon Foundation, books in the series have been reissued in new paperback and open access digital editions. For a complete list of books visit www.uncpress.org.

Ballad of the Buried Life

RUDOLF HAGELSTANGE

TRANSLATED BY HERMAN SALINGER

WITH AN INTRODUCTION BY CHARLES W. HOFFMAN

UNC Studies in the Germanic Languages and Literatures
Number 38

Copyright © 1962

This work is licensed under a Creative Commons CC BY-NC-ND license. To view a copy of the license, visit http://creativecommons.org/licenses.

Suggested citation: Hagelstange, Rudolf. *Ballad of the Buried Life.* Translated by Herman Salinger. Chapel Hill: University of North Carolina Press, 1962. DOI: https://doi.org/10.5149/9781469658285_Hagelstange

Library of Congress Cataloging-in-Publication Data
Names: Salinger, Herman.
Title: Ballad of the buried life / by Herman Salinger.
Other titles: University of North Carolina Studies in the Germanic Languages and Literatures ; no. 38.
Description: Chapel Hill : University of North Carolina Press, [1962]
  Series: University of North Carolina Studies in the Germanic Languages and Literatures.
Identifiers: LCCN UNK81010792 | ISBN 978-0-8078-8038-8 (pbk: alk. paper) | ISBN 978-1-4696-5828-5 (ebook)
Classification: LCC PD25 .N6 NO. 38

The English translation of "Ballade vom verschütteten Leben" by Rudolf Hagelstange is printed here with permission of the Hagelstange Estate.

Life is a series
of deaths and resurrections
Romain Rolland

TRANSLATOR'S NOTE

In presenting this translation of Rudolf Hagelstange's already famous *Ballade vom verschütteten Leben,* which won the *Kritikerpreis* a decade ago, my personal thanks are due and overdue in several quarters. First, to Rudolf Hagelstange himself for his encouragement of my efforts and for his appreciation and approval of the result, despite what I myself recognize as many shortcomings. Secondly, to the Insel-Verlag, Wiesbaden, whose interest was already manifested in the publication of Part VII of my translation in the *Insel Almanach auf das Jahr 1959,* for authorization to publish this English version and, what is equally appreciated, for kind permission to juxtapose the original German text of the *Ballade:* a feature which, I think, adds immeasurably to the whole.

Furthermore, I should like to thank Professor Charles Wesley Hoffmann of the University of California (Los Angeles) for his willingness to contribute his excellent introductory essay: an empathetic analysis which the translator has admired since it first appeared in *The Germanic Review* for April, 1958; likewise the editors of *The Germanic Review* and the Columbia University Press for their allowing us to reprint the essay here in slightly revised form. Professors Walter Kaufmann of the Department of Philosophy, Princeton University, and Frank Wood of the Germanic Languages Department of the University of Minnesota, both of them sensitive critics and able translators, have read my work in manuscript and were kind enough to make some valuable suggestions, many of which I was able to incorporate into the printed version.

Finally, I wish to thank my daughter, Jill Hudson Salinger and my secretary, Rosalinde W. Dole, for many hours of patient clerical and secretarial assistance; Professor Frederic E. Coenen and the other members of the Publication Committee of the University of North Carolina Studies in the Germanic Languages and Literatures, for enthusiastic support of my endeavors; and the Duke University Council on Research (especially its chairman, Professor John Tate Lanning) without whose confidence in the form of financial aid it would not have been possible for this book to see print.

H. S.

Durham, North Carolina
13 February 1962

INTRODUCTION[1]

The voice of Rudolf Hagelstange (b. 1912) has been a familiar one in Germany since the appearance in 1946 of his first major work, the *Venetian Credo*. This cycle of thirty-five sonnets, which had been completed a year and a half earlier and which circulated secretly before the end of the war, was written as an attack against the Third Reich. In the poems Hagelstange described the moral bankruptcy which, he felt, had made the Nazi evil possible, and he depicted man's return to the lasting values and goals of the spirit as the only means for overcoming the crisis. His sonnets, unlike many of those that flooded Germany in the postwar months, were carefully constructed and spoke with calm, artistic force. The *Credo* was soon recognized as one of the significant documents of the literary opposition to Hitler and its author as a lyric poet of great promise.

Since 1946 Hagelstange has done much to fulfill this promise. His poetry has appeared in collections as well as separately in newspapers and periodicals; and he has written literary and cultural essays, shorter prose pieces, and — most recently — a prize-winning novel. Equally far removed in his philosophical orientation from the Pandean rhapsodies of Germany's nature poets (Wilhelm Lehmann, Günther Eich, Karl Krolow) and the "nihilistic aestheticism" of Gottfried Benn and his followers, Hagelstange has devoted his attention to man, to the nature of man's being, and to the specific problems of existence in the chaotic world of today. In many ways the general attitude of his work is traditionalistic. For although he has moved away from the *Credo's* explicit call for a return to the ideals of German Classicism, he has continued to cite the validity of traditional humanitarian and Christian values in a world beset by modern problems. On the other hand, he is keenly aware of the threat that contemporary events pose for such values; and the marked optimism of his early verse has been replaced by a more skeptical appraisal of man's spiritual vigor. Where his message had earlier been openly didactic, his artistic purpose now seems to be the more modest one of describing modern experience and interpreting its significance.

---

[1] By kind permission of the editors of the *Germanic Review* the "Introduction" is reprinted substantially from my article in the issue of April, 1958.

We are, he claims in a figure that finds frequent expression in his work, beings placed in a nether region "between the star and dust". We have been brought into ever closer contact with the dust; and our view of the star, though its light is still visible, has become clouded.

It is with this brief sketch of Hagelstange's development and position in mind that one must approach the *Ballad of the Buried Life*. First presented to the public in a radio version, the poem in its slightly longer printed form earned for Hagelstange one of the important "German Critics' Prizes" for 1951-52; and along with the *Venetian Credo* it represents the highpoint of his creation thus far. Its story is told with imagination and moves at a pace of epic breadth and calm. And in his sensitive handling of the strongly dactylic free verse, the metric pattern in which most of the poem is written, Hagelstange demonstrates that he is a master of form and rhythm. [2]

The source for his *Ballad* is an Associated Press dispatch from June 17, 1951, which is reproduced at the beginning of the book. This news item provides the plot for a narrative poem told in ten cantos of varying length. More important, it provides Hagelstange with an effective symbol. For his *Ballad,* on the surface simply an imaginative recounting of the bunker experience of the trapped men, is actually an expression of the tensions and emotions and paradoxes of man's being and specifically of modern man's being. [3]

The ten main cantos are preceded by an introductory section that suggests the ideological background against which the story is to play: man and the things of his world are but conglomerates of dust "held in cohesion a modest space of time by that tension midway between ferment and decay". Whether with the normal speed of organic processes or in a few seconds as in war, they must again return to dust. "All is dust", so the passage begins; and it ends with an identification of the tale to follow as "the new saga of dust". The bunker experience, that is, simply represents a unique contemporary statement of this essential nature of being.

Much of the actual narrative of the *Ballad* is told in the first five cantos. After a panoramic glimpse of the German flight before advancing enemy armies, the six soldiers are introduced. Led by clerk they look

---

[2] For further brief description of the poem's form the reader is referred to page 92 of Hans Fromm's article "Die Ballade als Art und die zeitgenössische Ballade" in *Der Deutschunterricht,* VIII (1956) 84-99. Fromm's principal interest is in the ways Hagelstange's "ballad" conforms to and differs from the ballad genre, as this genre has traditionally been defined.

[3] The authenticity of the AP story has been strongly questioned, and Hagelstange underlines the symbolic nature of his poem when he admits that he too doubted the veracity of the report. However, he continues, it was as "paradigm" and not as fact that the incident appealed to him.

for the underground storage bunker where they hope to find not merely food and drink but also refuge from the senseless destruction of the last war days. Scarcely have they entered it, however, when a bomb springs the trap into which they have walked and buries them. Once candles have been found, the men, forgetting their predicament, fall upon the rich provisions and liquors piled high around them. Later, when their orgy is over, they fire cartridges to summon help and examine every possible avenue of escape. With the realization that they are entombed their earlier joy at discovering the bunker gives way to terror and despair.

In the fourth canto one of the men emerges as an individual personality. Young, awkward, acquainted with life only through books, "Benjamin" is the first to break under the strains of bunker life. His sheltered existence has not prepared him for this trial; and he is unable to resolve the contradiction between the world as it exists in his imagination and the fearful reality into which he is now thrust. Tormented by nightmares and the never-ending direct contact with the others, he seeks peace by shooting himself. Now death has entered the bunker, and the fifth canto depicts the effect death's presence has on another of the men. Sergeant Wenig has taken part in the liquidation of Jewish women and children at Saporoschje. The memory of this crime has tortured him for some time; but, seeing in it merely the execution of an order, he has been unable to admit his own culpability. Now he realizes that this is not the issue. Benjamin's suicide enables him to grasp the full significance of death for the first time, and for the first time he becomes completely aware of the fact that he has destroyed human life. This guilt, even though he was forced to assume it, he now recognizes as his personal responsibility; and his sense of justice allows only one thing. With his service pistol he kills himself, thus paying "the balance outstanding".

The sixth canto brings a lyrical pause in the narrative. Even in the preceding sections the poet has interrupted his story with metaphoric passages and philosophical asides. But here the sequence of events is almost completely abandoned, and the canto describes a dream of the carpenter Kuno. On a green meadow Kuno encounters his younger self and together the two wander off in search of "the world". The child-self picks a dandelion gone to seed; and, while the other self examines the marvelous, fragile construction of the white head, the flower is expanded into the cosmos and Kuno is swallowed up in it. Upon awakening, he tells this to the others, who discuss the vision and their own dreams with a mixture of mockery and reverent longing. The significance of the canto will be examined later; but Hagelstange himself has suggested its structural function in the story: [4] for the remaining men the

---

[4] "Die Form als erste Entscheidung" in *Mein Gedicht ist mein Messer,* ed. Hans Bender (Heidelberg, 1955), p. 40. The present study is indebted to this description by the poet of the *Ballad's* inception and of some of its formal considerations.

actual past has lost all meaning, and only in the form of the dream are they now able to conceive of the real world of color and light and natural growth above them.

Canto VII, an even more marked pause in the narrative, contains a discussion of time and, with this, one of the important keys for understanding the *Ballad*. As far as its role in the plot development is concerned, however, it simply emphasizes further the degree to which the entombed men have been cut off from normal existence. Now that their last timepiece has stopped, time is no longer a meaningful measure for the passage of life. Outside the bunker it is an external something to be escaped or pursued, wasted or saved; for these men it is a primitive inner experience. Unable to remember a past and without hope (i.e., belief in a future), they are aware only of an eternal present. Theirs is a life reduced to its absolute temporal essence as a progression of single moments.

In the next two sections the story again moves forward. Christopher is a Catholic, and the months in the bunker have been made easier for him by his faith in a stern but just God-Father and a suffering Brother-Christ. Altough he longs for rescue, he has presumed a divine purpose for his entombment; he has accepted it as God's will and has submitted to that will. Now he is paralyzed by disease and dies a slow, painful death; yet his death is not like that of Benjamin or Wenig. A mighty vortex of light is in Christopher's emaciated body; and as the other men minister to his needs, they become aware of human emotions long forgotten. This influence is short-lived, however, and the hopeless monotony of bunker life soon returns. It is broken only by two more events, the first of which is the sudden, violent death of the clerk. He has avoided the spiritual questions raised by the others and has concerned himself only with the satisfaction of his physical wants. He has sought escape in constant drunkenness and now is swept away by sickness as if by a typhoon. His end is that of an animal, and Hagelstange uses only twelve lines to describe it. The second event is the burning of the last candle. Up to this point (Canto IX) the constantly burning candles have provided the men, even at times of greatest despair, with a faint symbol of the light above. Now all "earthly contours" are wiped out, and the two remaining soldiers are creatures of a primeval darkness. Only the flowing of blood through their bodies still links them to the "dark tide" of life.

In the final canto Hagelstange discards the realistic narrative technique employed more or less consistently thus far. Of the surviving men, only Kuno has played a role in the story. The other has remained nameless; and now, in order to force the reader to identify himself in the closest possible manner with the bunker experience, the poet says that this last prisoner is none other than the reader himself! Thus it is the reader who is told here in Canto X that he has been buried, forgotten, reduced to a state of existence "by one sigh richer than the dust from which he came". It is the reader for whom the heartbeat becomes the only perceptible proof of his continued being. And it is the reader who is then led once more into light when this beat turns into the sound of the rescuer's spade. With the rescue and the collapse of Kuno, for whom the sudden light is too great a shock to bear, the plot of the *Ballad* ends.

The last canto is followed by a brief concluding passage in which Hagelstange returns to the ideological background of his poetry and which provides a final hint as to its deeper meaning.

From the first Hagelstange intimates that he is doing more than just telling a story. Before the narrative begins he acquaints the reader with the symbolic nature of the tale to follow, and he frequently pauses to comment on the events taking place. Yet one must guard against finding a single "moral" for the poem. Into the subject matter provided by the short AP dispatch the author has woven many themes, and his *Ballad* is a texture rich enough in motifs to stimulate the widest play of the reader's imagination. There is an overall pattern in this texture, however; and the pertinence of the single ideas, many of which are developed briefly and then apparently dropped, becomes evident once it is perceived. The central pattern has already been suggested: for Hagelstange the bunker is a "stage of suffering" representing the earth itself, and in the ordeal of the buried soldiers he sees a fitting symbol for the drama of human existence. [5]

Upon a first reading, and especially in the initial cantos, the reader is tempted to find a more limited message in the *Ballad*. The opening lines set the beginning of the action in the German catastrophe of 1945; the six men are introduced not simply as German soldiers but as six typical German soldiers chosen at random from the fleeing army; and — more important — there are motifs that can be explained best if the poetry is seen specifically as an allegory of *German* experience in the postwar years. Like postwar Germany, the bunker is buried under rubble and cut off from the rest of the world with which it once had connection. Like many Germans, the men feel that the event which isolated them signifies a total break with the past; and the disappearance of hope from the bunker indicates their growing distrust of the future. The constant presence of suffering here, the physical hardships of winter, the psychological strains resulting from lack of privacy, the heavy toll taken by disease, and the extraordinary proximity of death all underline further

---

[5] It is interesting to note in connection with this "stage" metaphor that Hagelstange first considered giving dramatic, not lyrical-narrative form to the bunker ordeal. The obvious dramatic potentialities of the fable have since been exploited by Margarete Hohoff in her play *Die Legende von Babi Doly* (Munich, [1956?]).

the similarity between the bunker situation and that of defeated Germany.

The clearest substantiation for such an interpretation is contained in the descriptions of the four deaths in the bunker. Although their episodes are not compared in any explicit way to the postwar German scene, Benjamin, Wenig, Christopher, and the clerk appear (in part) to represent attitudes that played conspicuous roles in the months after surrender. Wenig — the most striking instance, since the problem that occupies him is plainly linked to Nazism — seems to stand for the conscience of a nation as it attempts to separate innocence from guilt, to determine the precise nature of its responsibility, and to discover ways of atonement. Benjamin's struggle resembles the dilemma of German youth which, in 1945, found itself in a completely unknown, menacing world; and it is not difficult to see the reactions of an entire generation in his bewilderment, fear, resentment, and despair. The clerk's turn to drunkenness as a means for evading thought, his search for escape at any price suggest still another reaction to postwar reality. And Christopher's attitude reminds one of an idea frequently expressed by German authors in the late forties: that for him who accepts the suffering and sacrifice of the moment as part of God's plan, they represent an exercise in the difficult virtues of humility and selflessness. Because Christopher's example awakens a spark of new hope in those around him, he also seems to symbolize the positive influence exerted by religious faith in the dark postwar world.

There are a few other passages in the poem that lend support to such an interpretation: for example, the contrast at the beginning of Canto III between nature's rapid recovery from war's devastation and the soldiers' inability to effect a similar recovery. But this path does not lead much further. After the initial cantos one forgets that the six men are Germans; and the more we read of the *Ballad* the more evident it becomes that this tale of lonely, threatened, seemingly hopeless, buried life stands not just for German experience but for contemporary existence in general. Yet even this interpretation puts the emphasis in the wrong place, since statement of life's meaning contained here has timeless validity for Hagelstange. The recent years of crisis have helped to form it and the statement is, thus, a "contemporary" one; but it defines something more basic.

The most striking aspect of this definition is its apparent bleakness. The reader who is familiar with Hagelstange's writing and is, therefore, acquainted with the frequent "dust" and "star" images will realize from the opening words that the negative pole of existence will occupy the foreground here. At first the poem was actually to have been called the *Ballad of Dust*. And the theme of man as a creature made of and returning to dust — stated explicitly in the introductory lines — is suggested again and again in the narrative. The men are covered with dust by the explosion that cuts off their escape; they sleep on sacks of dusty meal; the rich food in the bunker becomes as tasteless as dust in their mouths; the wick of each candle finally falls to dust at their touch; and they bury their dead under flour with the words "to dust thou shalt return".

Although it indicates the poet's preoccupation with life's transitoriness, this motif in and of itself need not signify a negative view of man's being. More important is the fact that the six soldiers do not play active roles in the bunker drama but are, rather, acted upon by forces which they are largely unable to resist. Even the action that precipitates their suffering, their entry into the bunker, is a step for which the men are only apparently responsible. Hunger and the threat of annihilation drive them here; Dante's "lasciate ogni speranza" stands as a warning above the door but is "illegible"; and the six are compared to mice caught in the trap of fate, later to mice with which the cruel "she-cat Destiny" plays. Hagelstange refers to fate elsewhere in the *Ballad*, but once the underground ordeal has begun he depicts more precise forces. Disease, physical suffering, and death are only the most obvious and most powerful of them. When the men realize that their yells and shots will not bring help, an "unfathomable silence" falls upon them; and from now on they sense the constant menace of a grave-like stillness. Soon after they are buried, they decide to keep watch over the burning candle so "that the iron-like blackness [might] not crush them completely". Later, as the supply of candles shrinks, this force threatens ever more ominously:

> In all uncertainty
> this much was sure: the blunted dark,
> that lay in wait
> and had to triumph, would
> plunge down on them and blind...

It is, of course, the phrasing of these lines ("lay in wait", "had to triumph", "plunge down on them") which is most important for showing the extreme vulnerability of the men in the bunker and the superior strength of that which confronts them.

Winter, one of their inexorable foes, is described in similar language:

> Like glowing lava
> the cold crept, scorning their defences,
> farther and deeper. They wrestled desperately
> against the implacable foe...

(Note the use in both these passages of a paradoxical element — "blind" used with "dark" and "like glowing lava" used with "cold" — to suggest further the enigmatic nature of these forces). To keep warm the men either bury one another in meal (again the dust motif) or slap their arms against their bodies; and the latter action Hagelstange depicts in a simile that clearly illustrates the manipulation of the soldiers by the force in question (here "the cold"):

> They often were like
> jack-in-the-boxes on the string of a
> cruel witch, gnomes under a spell,
> whipped into an involuntary dance.

Fear, which at first filled the bunker "slowly, as with gently flowing water," seems to assume corporeal reality as its attack becomes more violent:

> But then anxiety
> suddenly stood at their backs,
> squeezing the throat, numbing the lung.

And still another, though less imaginative, example of this sort of wording appears in the description of monotony:

> Monotony,
> the butcheress of souls,
> silently did her bloody work.
> The victims remained
> in her power.

(It should be noted that by this time — Canto IX — Hagelstange has abandoned his flowing free verse with its elegiac undertone in favor of a more monotonous, essentially iambic cadence. This change occurs at Christopher's death, when the two remaining men are delivered over once and for all to the "butcheress of souls", monotony.)

Under the buffeting of such hostile forces the men in the bunker suffer a general spiritual dissolution and complete loss of self. When they come in search of food and refuge, they are typical individuals with normal desires, reactions, and emotions. At the end of the poem the survivors are scarcely distinguishable from the dead. They have been reduced to the last possible essence of being. Hagelstange's *Ballad* is, thus, a description of human regression, and each of its episodes is a station in this dissolution.

The realization that rescue can come only from above (Canto III) is an important first step, since in recognizing this the men admit that they are no longer able to determine the course of their own lives. Here only the way of Benjamin and Wenig is left for him who demands an active part in shaping his destiny, and the suicides mark the disappearance from the bunker of this function of normal living. Something else also passes with Benjamin and Wenig: the ability to remember. They alone retain conscious ties with the actual past; and once they have been destroyed (in a sense by these very ties) all awareness of the past vanishes. More significant, the process of memory itself now ceases to take place, and Kuno's dream illustrates this. Although Kuno "remembers" his child-self, he does so in the unreal atmosphere of a dream; and afterwards he cannot recall for his companions when or where the imagined experience occurred. The world of perceivable phenomena, which man normally uses to give perspective to his own existence and from which the soldiers have been cut off by the explosion, now lacks even the subjective kind of reality afforded it by memory.

The next step in dissolution is the change that the men's conception of time undergoes when the last watch stops. Their digestion, the growth of nails and hair still offer a feeble measure of time's passage. But "past" and "future" are now meaningless terms for them, and their time sense has become that of an animal which can comprehend only the single moment of the present. The fact that the remaining four victims go into a sort of hibernation during winter further indicates their regression toward an animal state, and Christopher's dying seems to call from them the last evidences of recognizable human emotions. Now only the final station, the extinguishing of the last candle, is left. When this has happened, the two survivors have ceased to exist as individuals. They are mere creatures, lost in an "eyeless silence" and aware of each other only when their hands meet. Because they perceive the beat of their hearts and the flow of their blood, they know they still live: but this is all that separates their life from death.

Hagelstange goes to great lengths to suggest how far-reaching and how complete a thing such spiritual degeneration is. Even before the last candle has burned down he tells the reader to "forget the image of the tree-trunk, fallen — anchored a while perhaps with just one root" if he wishes to know how close the men are to the boundary between being and not-being. And then in Canto X he seeks to demonstrate the full import of this final state of bunker existence by making it a part of the reader's own experience. You must go down into the bunker alone, he says, and you need bring nothing but "your old blindness". You must let yourself fall into blackness. You must invite despair and everything else that stalks you to feed upon your heart:

> Let them suck,
> until there's blackness in it: blackness, cold.
> It *can* not be more black nor colder than
> this night of shadowless shadows.

You must forget the concept of identity, and you must forget that "someone above" has forgotten to wait for you. Only then, the poet says, is the reader ready to assume the role of the sixth man in the bunker:

> And when you've quite forgotten, what you once
> thought that you knew and only are
> by one sigh richer than the dust
> from which you came: then, — then —
> you are like the other,
>
> YOU ARE THE OTHER,
> who with the carpenter walks through the dust.
> Then you two squat there, already kindred spirits
> with those four others, whom the flour's dust
> took in the form in which they went.

A great deal more might be said about the process of dissolution; but here — where the symbolic narrative and what it stands for become one — the true meaning of Hagelstange's poetry is revealed. By bringing the reader into the bunker the poet indicates his belief that the reader too is cut off from a world that once had value, threatened by forces he cannot resist, and reduced to a selfless component of life's "dark tide". Like the sixth man whose place he takes, he has been brought to the "zero point" of existence. Thus, the *Ballad's* statement of life's significance seems grim indeed. To be sure, there are a few moments in the narrative when light breaks through the bunker's darkness, when hope and positive meaning are still present. Kuno's dream, for example, signifies loss of contact with the real world, yet it also brings a fleeting vision of cosmic harmony in the lowly dandelion. Kuno is "indescribably filled with light", though this soon passes. Spring, which follows the dark and fearful winter, stirs in the men a modest hope "for a favorable juncture of fate, for a secret plan of the timeless powers". And in his suffering Christopher sends out such light that the candle beside him is "suctioned away by [the] invisible shining" of his soul. These evidences of light, the poet feels, must be included if the tale of buried life is to be an accurate symbol. Yet they do not halt the process of regression or seriously modify Hagelstange's bleak appraisal of earthly existence. There is no illumination whatsoever in the world of dust the reader enters.

Of course, the *Ballad* does not end with the reader's descent into the bunker. Along with Kuno he is "called out once more from dust's grim night into the light"; and it might be argued that here the zero point is overcome. This is true but only in a very special sense, for the final rescue must not be accepted at face value if Hagelstange's message is to be understood correctly. Release does not make the bunker experience any less real, and it does not negate what has already been said about life's meaning. "Oh! do not believe in rescue as you think it", the poet

warns the survivors as the first crack appears in the bunker wall. The
glance they must now meet is not that of human rescuers, but a divine,
cosmic glance. The light that now awaits them is not the daylight that
illuminates man's normal existence, the daylight his eye perceives
mechanically and uncomprehendingly. It is light which transcends this
and which one beholds with his entire being:

> Your eye,
> this needle eye, has threaded days and days
> like a child, embroidering a cloth or towel,
> a trembling monogram,
> stitch after stitch. Now however wait
> this-side and that-side of your own eyes' light,
> not sliced to yesterday, today, tomorrow, —
> oceans of timeless light. Entire light.
> The light.

This is light which comes at the instant when man recognizes that his
threatened and transitory earthly life is but a part of a larger, eternal
order of existence:

> — the light, that there within
> breaks open,
> like licking flames, enkindled
> against the All, that meets you
> in lightning-blaze, in which both life and death
> are gathered, glorified, and raised.

The rescue Hagelstange means is simply the advent of such light. It is
a moment when man is liberated from the blindness he suffers as long
as he sees in his temporal existence the whole truth about life. In Kuno's
case it is quite literally the moment of release from mortal blindness, for
he collapses when the light breaks in upon him. Unlike Kuno, the reader
is restored to the sphere of everyday living, but this is little more than a
necessary step for bringing the symbolic narrative to a close. There is no
indication that he returns to a life which has changed for the better or
that his bunker experience has given him the power to resist the forces
menacing him. Indeed, he has learned that humility before them is
perhaps the most realistic attitude human beings can attain. But he has
penetrated to the "roots" of existence (an image used several times in the
poem); and this has brought a new awareness of life's full import. He
has seen how quickly he can be reduced to the dust from which he was
shaped, yet he now recognizes that this process follows a law of being that
is all-inclusive and eternal. His rescue, like Kuno's, is the approach of
such recognition.

The short, concluding section of the *Ballad* summarizes all this, and in the poem's last lines Hagelstange states his belief that the law of being is directed, ultimately, toward a positive goal:

> Thus runs the new legend, the legend of dust;
> only the old is of eternal light. Long
> we wait — a life-long, — to read in it.
> Now the dust rises up, clouds and whirls down,
> covers the dust-formed Adam, throws him
> back into nothingness and lets him rest.
> Then light calls, generation after generation,
> the unborn, the lost that they beget
> from thousand darkened silences at last
> one single child of light.

Faith in a positive purpose for man's existence characterizes all of Hagelstange's writing, and the fact that the purpose is not further defined suggests that the faith is more important than the goal itself. There is some indication that the "child of light" should be seen as a Christian motif. (Indeed, it is not impossible to interpret the entire *Ballad* as a story of the pilgrimage through life's dust to a Christian salvation after death).[6] This, however, is certainly only one possible interpretation. The "child" seems to be merely the symbol for an ultimate end that must exist, but that mortals cannot know or describe more precisely. The connotations of the world "child" — purity, the promise of future growth and strength, humility — provide hints about the nature of Hagelstange's faith. But the knowledge that the eternal cycle of life and death is directed toward a positive goal is all that matters.

CHARLES W. HOFFMANN

University of California, Los Angeles

---

[6] In her *Welterlebnis in deutscher Gegenwartsdichtung* (Nürnberg, [1956]), for example, Inge Meidinger-Geise calls the work a "hymn of salvation" and sees in the "eternal light" of the final section a strictly Christian symbol (p. 284). Influenced apparently by existentialist interpretation, she claims that Hagelstange's definition of life's meaning "leads either to the abyss, to dust—or to the invisible, to the hand of God;" the choice depends on the personal belief of the individual reader (p. 285).

Warschau, 17. Juni 1951 (AP). — Polnische Arbeiter bargen in diesen Tagen bei Aufräumungsarbeiten an einem unterirdischen Bunker in Babie Doly bei Gdingen zwei Männer, von denen einer nach wenigen Schritten, die er im Tageslicht getan hatte, tot zusammenbrach. Sie waren die letzten von sechs deutschen Soldaten, die Anfang 1945 in einem riesigen Vorratsbunker der damaligen deutschen Festung Gotenhafen durch eine Sprengung von der Außenwelt abgeschnitten worden waren.
Der unzerstörte Luftschacht des Bunkers und die großen Lebensmittelvorräte hielten die Eingeschlossenen am Leben.
Die Berichte sprechen davon, daß zwei der Eingeschlossenen bereits nach kurzer Zeit Selbtsmord begangen haben. Von den vier übrigen wurden zwei krank und starben.

Warsaw, 17 June 1951 (AP). — Polish workmen, in clearing away rubble from the vicinity of an underground bunker in Babie Doly near Gdingen, recently dug up two men, one of whom — after a few steps taken in the light of day, collapsed and died. They were the last survivors of six German soldiers who, early in 1945, had been cut off from the outside world when buried in a gigantic supply-bunker of the German fortification "Gotenhafen" by an explosion. The undamaged air-shaft of the bunker and the large supplies of provisions kept the buried men alive. According to the reports, two of the men committed suicide after a short time.
Of the remaining four, two took sick and died.

Alles ist Staub. Da sind nur Stufen.

Eisen und Fels und der mürbe Boden,
den dein Spaten aushebt, das feste
steinerne Haus und die Hütte aus Lehm,
zerriebenes Korn, der gebrannte Teller,
von dem du dein Brot ißt;
Staub der Zahn, der es mahlt; die lästige Notdurft.
Staub dein Leben und Fleisch, untermischt
mit Wasser, viel Wasser, und —
gar gebacken vom Licht, von der Hitze
glutenden Sterns, zusammengehalten
eine bescheidene Weile von dieser Spannung
zwischen Gär'n und Verfall,
zwischen Dürsten und Stillung.
Staub, aufstiebend im Lichte und funkelnd
wie die Fruchtung von Blumen im Frühling
oder der silbrige Puder auf Schmetterlingsflügeln;
müder, erblindeter Staub im Dämmer von Böden und Kellern;
wesender Staub in sechs eichenen Brettern,
sechs Fuß unter dem Lichte.
Da sind nur Stufen.

Trotzdem gefällt es zuweilen dem Staube,
aufzustehen gegen den Staub. Dann hassen
Fleisch sich und Fleisch. Paläste
werfen sich über die Hütten. Das Eisen
dringt in die Ruhe des Steins.

All is dust. There are only stages.

Iron and cliff-rock and the ripe ground,
lifted by the spade, and the firm stone-built
house and the hut made of clay,
the ground grains of wheat, the fire-baked plate
from which you eat your daily bread;
dust is the tooth that grinds it. The faeces,
life and the flesh are dust, intermingled
with water, much water, and then
baked to a turn by the sun, by the heat
of that glowing star, held in cohesion
a modest space of time by that tension
midway between ferment and decay,
between thirst and its quenching.
Dust, dusting up in the sunbeam and sparkling
like the pollen of blossoms in spring or the silvery
powder on wings of the butterfly, membranous;
tired, blinded, the dust in the dusk of attics and cellars;
dust that decays between six oaken boards, too,
six feet under the sunlight.
All are but stages.

Nevertheless it pleases the dust
now and again to rise against dust. Then
flesh hates flesh. And palaces
hurl themselves over huts. And iron
thrusts into stillness of stone.

Unreifes Korn stirbt unter den Tritten
kriegender Heere. Schüsseln und Teller zerbrechen,
Zähne und Wirbel... Die ganze
leise und lüsterne Spannung zwischen den Dingen
springt mit einem einzigen Ruck aus den Angeln,
ballt sich zum Knäul, zu einem
berstenden Kern von Atomen und treibt
alles Gehaltene irr auseinander. Am Ende
ist da ein Staub, derselbe,
der einmal war, einmal sein wird.
In ein paar Tagen, Wochen und Jahren
haben sich Metamorphosen eines Jahrhunderts vollzogen.
Eisen stirbt schneller und kehrt
in die Erde zurück. Mörtel stirbt schneller.
Fleisch verbrennt in Stunden, Sekunden.
Rost und Asche und Moder, —
ach, welche Eile...

Hört denn die neue Sage vom Staube,
sechs oder sechzig Fuß tief unter dem Lichte.
(Unter dem Lichte ist tausend gleich eins.)

Green corn dies under the footbeats
of warring hosts. Bowls and pottery plates
shatter — and teeth and spines break. All the
light and lustful tension between things
jumps with a jerk from tense hinges,
clenching into a snarl, to a bursting
kernel of atoms and driving
all that once held wildly apart. And at last,
at last there's a dust, the same dust is
as it was in the beginning and shall be.
In a few days, in the weeks, in the years
the metamorphoses of a century round out.
Iron dies quicker and turns
back to the earth. The mortar dies quicker.
Flesh burns up in hours, in seconds.
Rust and the ash and the dry-rot, —
oh, in what hurry...

Hear now the new saga of dust,
six or sixty feet deep from the sunlight.
(Under the sun a thousand is one.)

I

Fünfmal war der Frühling vergeblich gekommen.
Der sechste war mächtig. Bäche
brachen verjüngt aus den Wäldern,
Bäche von Schweiß aus den Achseln
flüchtender Männer, Tränenbäche
aus den Augen der Fraun und letzte
Rinnsale Bluts aus noch winterlich hassendem,
tauendem Fleisch der Kinder des Staubes.

Hier noch und dort
trieben, wie Schollen Eises,
versprengte Armeen im Golfstrom des Sieges;
Schollen, bemannt mit Enterbten, Verdammten,
an die Schlacht wie an eine Galeere gefesselt,
die leck ist: Kinder,
die ihr Geschlecht noch nicht kannten,
alte Männer, die jetzt ihres Gartens gedachten,
wahllos zusammengewürfelte Haufen, einig
nur im gemeinsamen Nenner: als Letzte
fordern zu müssen, was schon verneint war.
Wähle aus diesen, wähle willkürlich
sechs und denke: sie haben
vor sich die frühlingsbewegte,
aber noch eisige See (schon Tausende
hat sie gefressen), im Rücken,
rückwärts *und* seitwärts den Feind.

I

Five times spring in vain had returned.
The sixth one was mighty. Brooklets
broke rejuvenated from forests,
brooklets of sweat from the armpits
of fleeing men, brooklets of teardrops
out of the eyes of the women, and final
tricklings of blood from the wintry and hating
thawing flesh of the children of dust.

Here yet and there yet
drifted, like driftblocks of ice,
straggling armies in victory's gulf-stream;
driftblocks manned by the damned, by the crews of
the disinherited damned, chained to battle
like galley-slaves chained to a leaking
galley: mere children
who did not yet know their sex,
old men who were thinking now of their gardens,
heaps senselessly thrown here together, united
only by one common mission: by being
the last ones who had to demand the already
denied thing. Choose from these at random
six and remember: they have here
the spring-shaken, still icy ocean before them
(thousands she's eaten already), behind them,
behind, beyond, on their flanks, too: the foe.

Sie haben
ein paar Schüsse im Gurt, zwei Pistolen.
Hinter ihnen, von rechts und von links,
rollen die Panzer; Geschütze und Bomber
halten Visier auf die Reste von Leben.
Und nun öffne,
wie zur Rettung, verstohlen den Ausweg.
Einer von ihnen,
ein Schreiber, weiß ihn. Verlaß dich
auf seine Weisheit. Er hat sie
über den Gaumen studiert,
schon in ruhigen Tagen. Manchmal
hat er Empfangenes quittiert (oder nicht).
Zu erinnern — welches Er-innern!
— brauchst du ihn nicht. Er hat schon
diesen Kitzel am Gaumen, der dicht vor dem Tode
noch die Greisin befällt. Eine Pfütze
künftiger Wollust bildet sich unter der Zunge.
Er winkt nur.

Warte geduldig. Sie finden
sicher den Weg und die Türe.
Ist hier nicht alles zu finden:
Deckung und Rast — und die Fülle
des Seltnen und Unverhofften,
Hades-kühlender Schatten,
Früchte des Paradieses..?
Sie treten, leichter atmend, erlöst fast
durch die nüchterne Pforte, darüber,

They have
still a few rounds in their belts and two pistols.
Back of them, out of the right and the left,
the tanks are rolling; the bombs and the bombers
are holding their sights on the remnants still living.
And now open,
as if toward rescue, the way out, in silence.
One of them knows it,
a clerk. You may trust in
his wisdom. He's studied it
over and over in quieter days. He
often has given receipts (or has he?)
for goods received. To remember him
isn't required. Already
he has that itch on his gum which comes over
old women close unto death. And a puddle
of future ecstasy trickles under his tongue-pit.
He only beckons.

Wait in patience. They're finding
safely, securely their way and their doorways.
Isn't everything here to be found —?
cover and rest and abundance
of rare things unhoped for,
shadows fit to cool Hades,
fruits out of Paradise...?
Breathing more lightly, almost saved,
they step through the simple, sober gateway,

unlesbar, die Inschrift vermerkt ist:
Lasciate ogni speranza...

Kisten sind da gestapelt, mit Kognak aus Cognac,
rotbraunem Medoc, Vin du Bourgogne,
die erlesensten Arten, Labsal für
Kronen und Päpste, eifersüchtig
gehüteter Schlaftrunk von ratlosen
Stabsoffizieren; Säcke aus Costa Rica,
Whisky aus London, Zigarrn, Zigaretten,
Fässer mit Schmalz und wagenrad-große
Käse; Konserven, Speckseiten — leise
schaukelnd im Luftdruck springender Bomben —,
zwei richtige Schinken... Dahinter,
wie ein Kugelfang gegen Hunger,
ungezählte Säcke mit Mehl,
weißem, staubigem Mehl, mehligem Staub,
Berge von Staub...

Eins, zwei, drei, vier, fünf, sechs Mäuse,
entronnen den mit Kadavern und Opfern
der Rasse gefüllten Trichtern und Gräben,
in einer riesigen Kammer aus Stahl und Beton
endlich geborgen! — mit sträubendem Barthaar
und fiebrigen kleinen Augen,
die Zunge zwischen den Schneidezähnen,
vor der Schlaraffen-Falle
des Schicksals. —

above which, illegible, stands the inscription:
ABANDON ALL HOPE, YE...

Cases are piled there, with cognac from Cognac,
ruddy-red Medoc, wine out of Burgundy,
the choicest vintages, balsam fit for
crowned heads and popes, a jealously guarded
sleeping potion for desperate
staff-officers; bags from Costa Rica,
whisky from London, cigarettes and cigars,
round vats of fat and big wheels of cheeses;
jellies and jams, rashers of bacon that
swing a bit as the bombs shake the still air,
two whole hams. And behind all,
like a magic spell against hunger,
countless sacks full of flour,
white, dusty flour, floury dust,
mountains of dust...

One, two, three, four, five, six mice, who
escaped from the ditches and shell-holes filled with the
race's cadavers and victims, now finally
safe in a giant chamber of concrete
and steel! — whiskers bristling they stand
with feverish small eyes,
their tongues between sharp incisors,
facing the paradise-baited trap
of destiny. —

Stiefeltritte. Krachende Kistendeckel.
Abgeschlagene Flaschenhälse, und glucksend
stürzt der Rausch aus den Flaschen. Eine
schmutzige Hand zieht ein Messer, säbelt
sechs halbpfund-schwere Scheiben von Schinken,
verteilt sie. (Indessen oben,
tausend, zwölfhundert Meter höher, eine
sauber gewaschene andere Hand
Bomben ausklinkt.) Und noch ehe
die ins Fleisch geschlagenen Zähne
den Fetzen an sich gerissen,
springt
die tödliche Feder vom Bügel,
„Klapp!" sagt die Falle und hat sie.

Manchmal bewegt ein Augenwink Gottes
Meer und Vulkane — leise, unhörbar;
aber das gellende, polternde Echo
vernimmst du.

Mitten im Biß hieb die Luft sie zu Boden.
Es tanzte der Bunker. Stahl und Beton
rissen gewaltig an ihrer Umarmung.
Zwei, drei aus der Reihe fallender Bomben
zerkrachten, zerspellten das feste Gefüge,

Boot-treads. Creaking covers of cases.
Knocked-off bottle-necks; gurgling,
drunkenness rushes out of the bottles. A
filthy hand draws out a knife and saws off
six heavy, half-pound slices of ham-butt,
doling them out. (Meanwhile, above them,
thirty-five hundred feet higher, a spotless
other hand, white and well-washed, releases
bomb after bomb.) And before the
teeth in the ham-meat, biting hard,
tear off a shred of it:
throbbing,
the fatal spring throbs and releases,
"Click!" says the trap. And the trap has them.

Now and again one lid-wink of God's eye
moves volcanoes and seas — inaudibly;
but the yelling, echoing thunder:
this you can hear.

In the midst of a bite and a swallow
air knocks them flat. The bunker is dancing.
Steel and concrete — closely embracing —
tug for a moment as though to let loose.
Two, three out of the stick of those falling
bombs burst open and opened the firm-built

begruben mit Bergen von Schutt und Gemäuer,
verbogenem Stahl und kittendem Erdreich
den Gang und die Pforte.

Leise schlug die zerrissene Luft
über dem Hügel zusammen, wie Wasser
über versinkenden Schiffen.
Unten, unter dem Hügel,
rieselte, wallte und schwebte
pudriger Staub durch die Kammer,
farblos im Dunkel, das wie ein Tuch
alles bedeckte, den Speck und die Mäuse, —
Staub von Gestern und Heute und Morgen.
Staub. Zeitloser Staub.

gateways and entrance and tumbled a wall down,
buried with mountains of twist-steel and earth-wall
gateways and entrance.

Now gently the torn air
closed again over the bunker, like water
closing over a sinking ship's hull.
Down below, under that hilltop,
trickled, floated and hovering sank
powdery dust throughout the chamber,
colorless there in the dark that blanketed
all like a cloth, both bacon and mice, —
dust out of yesterday, now and tomorrow.
Dust. Timeless dust.

II

Manchmal beliebt es der Katze Schicksal,
Großmut zu lügen. Satt, überfressen an
billigem, stündlichem Tod,
schleppt sie ein mageres, todwundes Leben
eine Weile zwischen den Zähnen umher,
gibt es — spielend — frei, und dann jagt sie's
wieder, betäubt es mit leichten Hieben der Pfote,
läßt es dann liegen, betrachtet
lüstern den zagen Aufstand der Kräfte,
Neugier und Laune zu schmecken
und Ängste des Opfers.

Also verfuhr es mit diesen. Sie fühlten
Staub in den Zähnen, im Nacken, auf aller
bloßen Haut ihres Leibes, der,
schwitzend in tödlicher Furcht,
bedeckt war mit sämigem Schleim;
Staub in den Lungen.
Sie rangen nach Atem,
nach Worten, gepreßten, nach Rufen, die taumelnd
— wie Vögel, verflogen ins Zimmer — sich stießen
an den kalten und fühllos schweigenden
Wänden des Bunkers.

Langsam, allmählich, wie bei Gestürzten,
sammelte sich ihr Bewußtsein. Stimmen
erkannten sich. Tastende Hände
sprachen einander Mut zu.
Ein Feuerzeug klickte. —

II

Often it pleases the she-cat Destiny
to pretend magnanimity. Full, overstuffed with
cheap and hourly death,
she drags some haggard, hurt-to-death being
around for a time, held between sharp teeth,
lets it sportively go, then hunts it
again, numbs it with paw-pats,
leaves it then lying, observes
lewdly the timid rousings of life-force,
sampling with exquisite curious caprice
the victim's anxieties.

Thus it happened to these. They could feel
dust in their teeth, at the back of their necks,
wherever skin of the body was bare,
sweating in deathly fear and
covered with viscous slime;
dust in the lungs.
They struggled for breath now,
for words, squeezed words, shouts that went reeling
— like birds in a room, lost — tumbling and thumping
on cold and unfeelingly silent
walls of the bunker.

Slow, by degrees, as in climbers who've fallen,
consciousness took shape. Voices
recognized voices. Groping hands
spoke courage to other hands.
A cigarette lighter clicked.

Immer noch nebelte Staub. Doch Konturen
zeigten sich schon. Ein Funke
Lichts sprang hell aus den Auge des Nachbarn.
Licht. Begnadetes Licht. Eine Stimme
sagte: Wir leben. — Und einer
klaubte ein Kerzenstümpfchen aus seiner Tasche.
Kerzen — sagte der Schreiber —, Kerzen
gibt es genug. Laßt uns suchen...

Wie durch die Wüste ein Veilchen
trugs einer ihnen behutsam voran.
Sechs gigantische Schatten in Bittprozession
hinter dem winzigen Docht.
Ach, wie er flackernd verging! Minuten
schien er bemessen. Sie suchten
mit brechenden Nägeln, blutenden Fingern
zwischen den Stapeln. Eine Kiste
französischen Kognaks, — nein, alle! —
boten sie für ein einziges Talglicht.
Eines nur. Oder ein halbes! Ein neues
Stümpfchen zum Weitersuchen! Ihr Leben
schien mit diesem zuckenden Dochte
gekoppelt.

Preise die Weisheit des Schreibers...
Nicht eines — Tausende fand er,
geschichtet in festen Kartons!
Tausende Stunden, Monate, Jahre
tröstlichen Scheines lagen gespart.
(Wer will sie verbrauchen...)
Sie schlugen sich auf die Schulter, umarmten
einander, küßten den Finder. Ein Taumel
kindischer Hoffnung machte sie schwindeln.
Atmeten ihre Lungen nicht leichter?

And dust-fog still sifted. Slowly some contours
started to show. And a spark
sprang from the eye of a neighbor, brightly.
Light. Blessed light. And a voice spoke,
said "We're alive". — And someone
dug up a candle-stump out of his pocket.
Candles — the clerk said — candles aplenty,
we've plenty of candles. Let's find them...

As through the desert a violet,
one of them bore it before them with care.
Six gigantic shadows in prayerful procession
behind the tiny wick.
Ah, how it flickered toward dying! Its minutes
seemed to be measured. They searched now
with cracking fingernails, bleeding fingers
between the stacks. A case of
cognac from France, — no, the whole lot! —
for one single candle of tallow.
One — or a half one! A new little
stump to go on searching! Their life seemed
tied to this wick,
trembling and twitching.

Praise the clerk's wisdom...
Not one — but a thousand he found,
piled in tight cartons!
Thousands of hours, of months, years
of consoling flow lay there, saved up.
(Who will consume them...?)
They clapped each other on the shoulder, embraced
one another kissing the finder. The magic
of childlike hope made them dizzy.
Didn't their lungs breathe easier?

Sicher gab es da Schächte, — Poren, mit denen
dieser Keller atmete, Lüftung empfing.
Schächte, aus denen man aufstieg,
Wenn das Desaster verraucht war.
Oben — wütete Mord und Verfolgung.
Hier unten war man doch sicher;
sicher und trefflich versorgt.
Kinderchen, hört auf den Schreiber:
Leben wir? — Gut. Also laßt uns
dieses Leben genießen! Morgen
sehen wir weiter.

Und nun betrachte das seltsame Schauspiel:
Wie sie Kerzen ringsum entzünden,
dreißig und vierzig still brennende Kerzen;
Kisten kanten, die festliche Tafel zu richten.
Einer schneidet aus einer Rolle Papier
ein sauberes Tischtuch. (Gemütlichkeit
schätzen die Deutschen.) Kanister
dienen als Stühle. Einer blickt auf die Uhr.
Die zeigt sechs. — Wir speisen zu Abend,
sagt geckig der Schreiber. Ich bitte
die Herren zu Tisch.

Sie trinken Burgunder: Nuits de St. George,
beginnen mit Salm bretonischer Herkunft.
Dann kosten sie endlich den würzigen Schinken.
Sie sind jetzt mäßig, bedenken das Nächste,
das Fleisch in den Büchsen. Und während sie speisen,
sorgt dieser und jener für wechselnde Mahlzeit.
Sie kosten und schmecken, verachten und loben.
Sie sprechen nachsichtig und beinah mitleidig
von ihren Herren, die längst schon verdauten,

Surely some shafts, — like pores, through which
this cellar was breathing, brought them fresh air.
Shafts, through which to ascend, when later
the smoke of disaster had dusted away.
Above, pursuit and murder were raging.
Here underground at least one was safe;
safe, well provided.
Listen, boys, it's the clerk who is speaking:
Are we alive? — Good. Then let us
enjoy this new life! Tomorrow
we'll see what comes next.

And now behold the strangest spectacle:
How they illumine the candles about them,
thirty, no forty hushed bright-burning candles,
tipped wooden cases to form festive board.
One, from a long row of paper, is cutting
a clean banquet-cloth (Gemütlichkeit
is prized by the Germans.) Canisters
serve them as chairs. One looks at the clock.
It points to six — We're dining this evening,
the clerk says, wise-cracking: Gentlemen,
please be seated.

They are drinking Burgundy: *Nuits de St. Georges;*
they start with salmon of Brittany,
then finally taste of the spicy ham.
For now they are moderate, think of what's coming,
the tinned meats. And while they are feasting,
each one takes thought of varied meals coming.
They taste, they smack lips, they scorn and they praise.
With near pity and gently, they speak of their masters
who long since digested such as what they're enjoying;

was sie hier genießen; entzünden Zigarren
und streifen das Bauchband
über die Finger. Der Korkenzieher
dreht still seine Runden; es mundet
der Kognak...

Wer hat die Tage gezählt, da ihnen
dieses versagt war? — Ein kurzer Urlaub,
einmal im Jahr (oder in zweien). Endlose Reisen,
sechs, sieben Tage im schmutzigen Zug, einen
Klumpen Butter im Bündel, und Flaschen mit
Wodka, drei oder vier, und Konserven —
Marschverpflegung, ersparte —
für den Hunger daheim.
Fahren, stehen und fahren, todmüde, — süchtig
nach einem leinenen Bett, nach Ruhe,
sauberen Hemden, gedeckten Tischen,
schmackhafter Mahlzeit; nach den
Augen der Kinder, den Armen der Frau.

Laß sie nicht denken... Immer
kamen sie doch zu kurz. Alarme
rissen sie aus dem Schlafe. Acht Tage
reichten die Büchsen, vierzehn
reichte die Butter. Dahinter
stand schon der Mann mit der Schere
und schnippelte an der gefelderten Karte.
Sieben Tage zurück — in die trostlose Weite,
an den blechernen Napf, in genagelte Stiefel.
Rückmärsche, länger und länger,
Rationen knapper und knapper, dazwischen
— Heister, koppheister! — ein blutiges,
atemberaubendes Tänzchen ums liebe,
leidige Leben...
Her mit dem wagenrad-großen gelben
Käse aus Sonstwo! Daumendick eine Scheibe!

they light up cigars,
and they fit the cigar-bands
over their fingers. The popular corkscrew
makes its slow turns; how good
is the cognac...!

Who had counted the days when all this was
denied them, — A short leave,
once in a year (or in two). Endless journeys:
six, seven days in a filthy train, a lump
of butter in a bundle, and bottles, and canned goods —
marching rations, saved up —
for the hunger at home.
Traveling, stopping and starting, tired to death, — longing
for a bed with bed-linen, for rest, for
clean shirts, covered tables,
meals that are tasty; longing after
the eyes of children, the arms of a wife.

Don't let them think... Always
they got the short end. Alerts
tore them up out of sleep. A week
the canned goods would last, two weeks
lasted the butter. Behind all waited
the man with the ticket-punch
snipping the sectioned card.
Seven days back — through disconsolate distance,
to the tin plate, into hobnailed boots.
Retreating marches, longer and longer,
rations tighter and tighter, and, in between-times,
— head-over-heels and heads up! — a bloody,
breath-taking dance for dear,
miserable life...
Pull down that yellow cheese, big as a wagon-wheel,
cheese from Somewhere! Slice it thick as your thumb!

Daumendick Butter darauf. Wir sitzen
wie die Made im Speck, die Made
will fressen.

Langsam verlöschen die Kerzen. Einer
taumelt empor; erbricht sich. Einer
sagt: Ich will schlafen. Einer
zieht eine Photographie, die Frau und zwei Kinder,
aus seinem Soldbuch. Einer
schreit: Wir müssen hier raus! Einer
sagt: Wir sind Idioten. Der letzte steigt
schwankend auf seinen Sitz, strafft sich,
reckt seinen Arm und lallt mit
brüchigem Hohne: Heil Hitler!

Die es vermögen, kippen und wälzen
ein paar Säcke mit Mehl, betten sich:
Staub auf den Staub.

Put thumb-thick patches of butter on top.
We're stuck here like maggots in bacon, and maggots
want to gorge themselves.

Slowly the candles die out. One fellow
stumbles to his feet; he vomits. Another
says: I'm for sleeping. A third
pulls out a snapshot: wife and two children,
out of his pay-book. A fourth man
screams: Let's get out of here! Another
says: We are crazy. The last one climbs
up on his chair, sways to "attention",
stretches his arm up and babbles in cracking
scorn: *Heil Hitler!*

Those who are able to, tip and roll
a few sacks of flour, bed themselves on them:
dust upon dust.

III

Oben
lächelt das Land aus verweinten
Augen und wäscht sich vom Blute.
Endlose Züge staubgrauer, stummer Kolonnen
sind nach Osten getrottet, und bunte
trällernde Vögel lösen sie ab, ein Nest sich
neu zu erbau'n, sich zu gatten,
Leben zu brüten, neues,
flaumzartes Leben in wüsten Provinzen, —
ähnlich dem Menschen. Winde haben
Samen geworfelt über den Schuttberg,
Quecke und Miere Wurzel geschlagen,
Grünes zu bilden, Hoffnung, allmählich,
Monat um Monat, ein wenig mehr
Grünes.

Doch unten,
unter dem Hügel, da Hoffnung
feil schien wie Speise, welkt nun
mit jedem verglimmenden Docht einer Kerze
und taumelt ein Blatt aus der grünen
Krone der Zukunft.
Längst ist der Atem
billig geworden, billig wie Mehl,
Kognak und Rotspon; wie der verrückte
Rausch — und nach ihm die stille Verzweiflung...
Diese Verzweiflung, die täglich
(aber nie tagt es) mit ihnen
aufwacht, grau wie der Dämmer,
der sie umgibt, monoton, die nur manchmal
jäh zu schrillem Geheule,
Flüchen und Vorwürfen anschwillt und gurgelnd
über dem Kopfe sich schließt, —

III

Above
smiles the land out of wept-out
eyes and wipes away the blood.
Endless processions of dust-gray, silent columns
have trotted eastward, and motley
trilling birds relieve them, to build
a new nest for themselves, to pair,
to breed life, new,
downy, delicate life in the waste-land provinces, —
like unto man. Winds have
shaken seeds over the rubble-mound,
quick-grass and pimpernel have taken root,
to form something green, like hope, gradually,
month after month, a little more
green.

But below,
under the hill, there hope
seemed cheap as supplies, withers now
with every dying wick of a candle
and lets fall one leaf from the greening
crown of the future.
Long since, their breathing
has become cheap, cheap as the flour,
cognac and claret; as the crazy
jag — and thereafter the quiet despair...
This despair, which daily
(though never it dawns) with them
awakens, gray like the twilight,
which yet surrounds them, monotonous, only at times
harsh as a shrill howl,
swelling to curses, reproaches, and closing
gurgling over their heads,—

und dann wieder, urplötzlich, zurücktritt,
gerade bis unter das Kinn.

Gnädige Tage, da sie noch glaubten,
Ausflucht zu finden. Sie waren
an das Verhängte gewöhnt. Und verschüttet
waren schon manche, lebendig begraben,
und gehen noch heut mit gebügelten Hosen
des Sonntags mit Frau und Kindern spazieren. —
Dieses schien leichter, beinah gefahrlos.
Luft war und Speise. Wo Luft ist, ist Hoffnung
auf einen Ausweg. Den würden sie finden,
heut oder morgen. Und was
sie nicht zwangen,
das schafften die draußen. (Schatzgräber
sind rührig.)

Bis sie begriffen.

Alles war da versucht. Keine Stelle
an dem Gehäuse, die sie nicht beklopften. Keinen
Spalt, in den sie den Keil nicht getrieben
wütenden Eifers. Keine Klappe,
die sie nicht tausendmal schon gelüftet!
Schwarze Kanäle in unergründliches Schweigen.
Anfangs verfuhrn sie behutsam —- aus Schläue;
schließlich mit Rufen und Schreien,
regelmäßig nach Uhrzeit bei Tage;
manchmal bei Nacht. Alle Patronen
(so hieß es) waren verschossen.
Donnernder Hall hier unten — von oben
leises Geriesel als wisperndes Echo.
Sie blieben im Schweigen.

Langsam, wie mit leise fließendem Wasser,
füllte die Angst den Bunker. Allmählich,
zentimeterweise, stieg der Gedanke,

and then, all of a sudden, retreating again
to just below the chin.

Happy days, while they still believed
they could find an exit. They were
used to disasters. And many a man
had been thus buried, buried alive,
who still today was walking about
with well-creased trousers Sundays with wife and children. —
This, their plight, seemed easier, almost without danger.
There was air, there were victuals. Where air is, there hope
exists for an exit. They would find one,
today or tomorrow.
What they failed to do,
the outside world would. (Treasure-
hunters are active.)

Till they understood.

Everything was tried. Not a place
on the walls of their house that they did not hammer.
Not a crack they did not drive a wedge into
with feverish zeal. Not a lid or trap
that they had not already lifted a thousand times!
Black canals into unfathomable silence.
At first they proceeded with caution — shrewdly;
at the last with shouting and screaming,
as a rule by day, according to clock-time,
often by night. All their ammunition
(it was said) had been fired.
Thundering noise here below — from above
a gentle trickle as whispering echo.
They remained in the silence.

Slowly, as with gently flowing water,
anxiety was filling the bunker. Gradually,
centimeter by centimeter, the thought was rising,

vergessen, verloren zu sein, an ihr Herz.
Einer verschwieg es dem andern. Witzelnd
suchten sie ihn zu verscheuchen.
Ferien vom Leben — sagte der Schreiber —
hat man nur selten. Tödliche wohl. Aber solche:
Essen und trinken und atmen —
nur auf Verdacht..! ? — Aber dann stand sie
plötzlich im Rücken,
drückte die Gurgel, lähmte die Lunge.
Ekel kroch aus den Speisen, Ekel
drang aus dem Winkel,
wo sie mit Mehl ihre Notdurft bedeckten.
Ekel stieg aus den Flaschen; denn Wasser
gab es nur Tropfen, hoch an der Decke.
(Zuweilen klomm einer hinauf und leckte
an dem kalten Beton.) Sie wuschen
manchmal die Hände mit Kognak;
manchmal mit Tränen.

Anfangs löschten sie nachts — wenn die Uhr
Nacht anzeigte — den Docht. Aber bald schon
hielten sie Wache, lösten einander
ab, wie einst droben,
daß sie die eiserne Schwärze
nicht vollends erdrücke,
schonten den winzigen Stein, den letzten
ihres Feuerzeugs, das der eine
sorgsam in seinem ledernen Beutel
auf seiner Brust barg.

Sonne ging unter und auf, und Mond schien.
Wolken wanderten still, oder Sterne
traten hervor aus der Nacht. Hier unten
war ein windloser Ort.

of being forgotten, lost, rising to their hearts.
One kept it hushed from the other. Joking,
they sought to scare it away.
Vacations from Life — said the clerk —
one gets 'em but rarely. Fatal ones, yes. But this kind:
eating and drinking and breathing —
only on suspicion...!? — But then anxiety
suddenly stood at their backs,
squeezing the throat, numbing the lung.
Disgust crept out of the food, disgust
rose out of the corner, where
they covered their faeces with flour.
Disgust climbed up out of the bottles; for water
existed only in drops now, high up on the ceiling.
(At times a man would climb up and lick
the cold concrete.) They often
washed their hands now with cognac,
often with tears.

At first they snuffed out the wick at night —
when the clock-hands pointed to night. But soon they
were keeping a watch up, relieving each other
as once up above,
that the iron-like blackness
not crush them completely,
saving the flint, the tiny last one
of their lighter, which one of them
wore with care on his breast
in a small leather purse.

Sun went down and came up, moon shone.
Clouds wandered silent or stars
appeared out of the night. Here, down below
was a place without wind.

Kerze auf Kerze
brannte, verzehrte sich still:
leises Versprechen zugleich und Sinnbild
niederbrennender Hoffnung.
Wer da wachte, der sah es,
wie ihr Leib sich verkürzte.
Schließlich blieb nur ein Rest
langsam verkohlenden Dochtes.
Zwischen den Fingern gerieben,
zerfiel er
zu Staub.

Candle after candle
burned, consumed itself softly:
Gentle promise and symbol at once
of hope burning lower.
Whoever held watch there, saw it,
saw how her body grew shorter.
At least there was only a remnant
of slowly blackening wick left.
Rubbed between the fingers,
it fell into bits:
into dust.

IV

Einer war da, ein Junger. Er hatte
Urlaub im Sommer gehabt und das erste
Mädchen geküßt. Seine Mutter
hatte nur diesen: verzärtelt, versponnen,
hoch aufgeschossen und immer verlegen,
wenn man ihn ansprach. Heimlich
las er verbotene Bücher. Er wußte
alles vom Leben — aus Büchern. Eben
hatt' er die immer stößigen Kniee
aus der Schulbank genommen, da hob ihn
der Krieg aus den Träumen. Acht Wochen
hatte er Griffe gekloppt und Spinde entstaubt,
Ehrenbezeigung erwiesen, als Längster
dünnes Kabel auf schwankender Stange
in die Bäume gefädelt; Drähte verknüpft.
Wie eine Scheuche im Feld für die Vögel
hatten sie ihn mit läppischem Spott,
Flüchen und Titeln behängt; Erlösung
schien ihm der Wechsel zur Truppe.

Dieser — Benjamin hieß ihn der Schreiber —
litt in den Träumen. Das Leben,
das aus den Büchern, schien ihn zu hänseln,
mit Nadeln zu stechen bis in das Mark.
Alles Erträumte verkehrte im neuen
Traume sich schrecklich. Er sprach nicht.
Aber sie hörten ihn schreien
immer des Nachts: wenn er ruhte,
kam ihm ein Alp. Und er baute
sich in der äußersten Ecke ein Lager,
verkroch sich. Wachend
schien er gefaßt und gefällig, fast mutig.
Aber da innen
wuchs ihm ein Tumor. Schweigend
litt ers im unterirdischen Tag; aber nächtlings,
wenn seine Scham sich befreite,
schrie ers hinaus.

IV
There was one there, a youngster. He had
had his furlough in summer and had kissed
his first girl. His mother
had only this son: pampered, protected,
shot up to great height and always embarrassed,
whenever you spoke to him. Secretly
he read forbidden books. He knew
all about life — from books. Straight
from the school-desk with his clumsy knees,
war lifted him from his dreams. Eight weeks long
he had manhandled the carbine and dusted the lockers,
given salutes and, as the tallest,
twisted thin wires on swaying crossbars
up in the trees, making connections.
Like some scarecrow in the field, they'd draped him
with ragged scorn, with curses and titles.
Like salvation to him
had seemed his transfer to combat.

This youngster (the clerk named him Benjamin)
suffered in dreams. The life he
had learned out of books seemed to be teasing him,
pricking with needles into his marrow.
All that he dreamed then made itself over
into a terrible new dream. He never
spoke to them. But they heard his screaming
always at night: whenever he lay down,
nightmare began and he constructed
his resting place in the outermost corner,
crawling into hiding. In waking hours,
docile he seemed and composed, almost cheerful.
But deep inside him
a tumor was growing. In silence
he bore it in the under-earth day; but nightwise,
when his shame was set free,
he screamed it abroad.

Anfangs
glaubte er, es zu verbergen, wenn er
Kerzenwacht hielte, freiwillig. Und gerne
nahmen sie's an. (Sie lebten noch immer
im Rhythmus des Lichts.) Aber bald schon
wollten sie's nicht. Er schrie dann bei Tage
schrecklicher nur und allen vernehmbar.
Eines Polypen
grausige Arme
sahen sie schlagen
hinten, im Dämmer,
wenn er sich wälzte
zwischen den Säcken,
allen den Jammer
jählings erbrechend,
den sie mühsam herunterwürgten.

Plötzlich begriff er die schreckliche Prüfung
menschlicher Nähe, diese bis auf die Haut,
bis in die fremden Leiber
dringende Schändung, nur tragbar
in der Betäubung der Wollust. Schamlos
schien ihm das Dasein, diese hier unten
wie in Spiritus künstlich erhaltne
Leibesgestalt des aufrechten Tieres,
das fortlebte im Schein, wie es oben
scheinbar gelebt; das Lüge lebte,
weil es Leben gelogen. Diesen
zwanzigfach und mehr gefalteten Darm,
der sie, wie ein satanischer Fühler,
in diese Höhle gewiesen.

In the beginning
he thought he could hide it, if he took on
candle-watch for them, volunteering.
They gladly accepted. (Still they were living
in the rhythm of light.) But very quickly
they had to refuse. He screamed then by day
only more awfully, heard by them all.
The horrible arms
of some kind of octopus
they could see twisting
back in the twilight
whenever he twisted
between the flour sacks,
suddenly vomiting
all of the misery
they painfully choked back.

On a sudden he grasped the terrible trial
of human proximity, that down-to-the-skin-line
and on, into strange bodies, pressing,
penetrating violation, bearable only
in the benumbing of lust. Existence
seemed to him shameless, here down below,
this artificially-kept bodily form
(preserved as in alcohol) of the upright beast,
living on by candlelight, just as it pretended
above in the sunlight; the Lie was living,
for it lived a belied life: this
twenty-fold and more folded-over intestine,
which, like a satanic antenna,
first pointed them their way to this hell-hole.

Jedes, was sie nun taten,
war eine Kränkung. Ihr Schmatzen
riß an den Nerven. Ihr Reden
brannte wie Phosphor in seinen Ohren.
Selbst ihr Trübsinn, der jähe Jammer
schienen ihm Auswurf, Abscheu erregend,
Unrat säuglingshaft kümmernder Seelen.

Manchmal, minutenlang
— wenn jene ruhten —
kam es ihm plötzlich wie Wunder der Heilung,
dachte er Daniels, jenes Propheten,
der in der Löwengrube noch heil blieb,
glaubte die Rettung.
Dann war ein Freund nah, oder die Mutter
winkte ihm zu. Das Mädchen vom Sommer
kam ihm entgegen, linkisch und lächelnd.
Bilder erstanden —
er hatte in Bildern, fremden, entliehenen,
immer gedacht — und wollten ihn halten...
Aber da regte sich einer der Schläfer,
grunzte und lallte. Es stoben die Schemen
schreckhaft davon; und Öde und Ekel
hockten im Winkel und fletschten
hohnvoll die Zähne.

Und eines Nachts — er saß bei der Kerze
wie jeder und alle; es dunkelten oben
schon Kirschen und Beeren —,
da wuchs das Entsetzen aus einer der Ecken
genau auf ihn zu, ganz langsam, behäbig
sich blähend, als blase
ein Kraftprotz vom Jahrmarkt
es pausbäckig auf, dahinten im Dunkel.
Da war sie, die gräßliche Drohung der Kindheit:

Everything that they did now,
to him was an insult. The smacking of lips
tore at his nerves. Their talking
burned in his ears like phosphorous flame.
Even their sadness, their sudden miseries
seemed to him garbage, exciting disgust,
filth of these suckling-like worrying souls.

Often, minutes on end
— when the others were resting —
it came to him quick like a miracle of healing,
and he thought of Daniel, Daniel the Prophet,
who remained whole in the den of the lions,
and he believed: rescue.
Then a friend neared him, or else his mother
beckoned and waved. The girl from last summer
came then to meet him, awkward and smiling.
Images, pictures —
always he'd thought in strange, borrowed pictures —
rose, tried to hold him...
But then there stirred one of the sleepers,
grunted and babbled. Like dust his illusions
blew frightened away; sterility, nausea
squatted in corners, baring and gnashing
great scornful teeth.

And once at night — he sat by his candle
like each man and all; above them were darkening
cherries and berries —,
suddenly terror grew out of one corner,
heading right at him, calmly
filling with air, as if being blown up
by a carnival strong-man
swelling his cheeks, back there in the darkness.
There stood the horrible threat of his childhood:

es schwollen die Dinge unkenntlich, es wuchsen
die Hand und die Nase; und riesige Füße.
Dann drehte das Rückgrat
sich wie eine Spindel,
und an ihr die Glieder.
Es fielen die Wände. Im Raum trieb der Raum.
Man konnte nicht schreien
und schrie doch, in Tränen gebadet,
nach Hilfe... und wurde gehört.

Hier aber saß er, den Knebel
fest auf der Zunge, das Wissen im Blute:
Keiner hört dich, erhört dich.

Er kannte, aus Büchern, die daumbreite Stelle.
Und die war zu treffen.

Er traf sie genau. —

Plötzlich war da ein Toter im Raum;
oder der Tod. Wer will das entscheiden...
Dieser war gnadelos tot. Nicht Bruder
war er, noch Vater. Solche
kann man begraben. Verwandte
kommen von weit; man muß ihnen schreiben,
Totenwäscher bestellen, den Text
einer Todesanzeige entwerfen, den Sarg
auswählen, die Grabstelle kaufen...
Ja, kaufen
muß man den unerbetenen Tod, bezahlen.
Mitten im grauen Gram der Verwaisten
klimpern lustig Dukaten und rascheln
sauer ersparte Scheine. Man muß
immerfort kaufen und immerfort laufen,
Briefe schreiben und Augen reiben,
Hände drücken und Kleider färben,
den Toten beerben.
Eins, zwei, drei Tage, und eh mans gedacht,
ist so ein Toter zu Grabe gebracht.

every thing swelled itself past recognition:
his hands and his nose; his feet were gigantic.
Then began turning
his spine like a spindle,
and on it his four limbs.
The walls started falling. Space writhed through space.
He could not cry out,
yet cried out, burst in tears,
cried for help... and was heard.

But here he was sitting, the gag firm,
firm on his tongue, aware in his blood:
Nobody hears you, no one will heed you.

He knew it from books: a thumb's breadth across,
the spot to be hit.

He hit it exactly. —

Suddenly a dead man was there in the room;
or it was death. Who can tell which is which?...
This one was dead as a doornail. No brother,
no father was he. Such
people one buries. Relatives, kinfolk
come from far off; you write them or wire them,
order the undertaker, the text
of a death-notice needs to be written, the coffin
must be selected, the lot must be bought...
Yes, bought
is the unasked-for death, purchased and paid.
In the midst of the gray grief of the bereft
coins rattle merrily, there rustle
banknotes earned in the sweat of the brow.
One must buy often and much, run errands and such.
There are letters to write and eyes to wipe,
there are hands to shake and clothes to dye,
and inherit death's dower before we die.
Before you're aware, two, three days have rolled round
and a dead man like this is safe underground.

Aber hier
war keine Erde, Benjamin zu bestatten.
Weder Sargtischler, Drucker noch Zeitung
konnten an ihm verdienen. Er war
so tot wie begraben, begraben wie tot.
Sie konnten ihn nicht abholen lassen.
Er blieb auch als Toter. Was wollte es wiegen,
daß sie am Morgen (auf den sie vergeblich
harrten) ein Vaterunser,
hilflos und stockend, heruntersprachen,
vier Sack Mehl auf ihn rinnen ließen:
stäubendes weißes Mehl; aber Staub.

Und einer sagte, ein Katholik:
In pulverem reverteris.

But here
there was no ground to bury Benjamin rightly.
Nor coffin-maker, printer, morning paper
to earn their due out of him. He was
as dead as if buried, as buried as dead.
They could not have him fetched and carried away.
He stayed there, a dead man. What could it count
that in the morning (they awaited it vainly)
they spoke the Lord's Prayer,
stammering, helpless,
and let four sacks of flour trickle down over him:
dusty white flour-meal; but dust.

And one of them said — a Catholic:
In pulverem reverteris.

V

Tote sind immer im Recht. Du redest
eine Stunde an einem Faden, und schließlich
glaubst du, alles bewiesen zu haben, —
da beginnen sie wieder zu schweigen.
Alles,
was du gesagt hast, is widerlegt.

Benjamin schwieg in der weiten Kammer. Es hallte.
Bescheiden, aber beharrlich und unübersehbar,
wartete er, so wie manchmal,
wenn das Schwurgericht tagt,
ein Zeuge auf einer Bank sitzt.
Drinnen, im Saale, flammen die Zungen.
Talare hängen gleich entliehenen Fahnen
um den gestärkten Kragen der Jurisprudenz.
Kläger, Beklagte spielen ihr Spiel. Ein jeder
hat seine Trümpfe und zieht sie.
Dann aber wird
der Zeuge, der letzte, gerufen. Er tritt
leise und zögernd ein in den Saal, — da
wirft der Beklagte die Karten, ergibt sich...

Zahllose Male
hatte der Wachtmeister Wenig
seine Karten gesteckt. Augen
hatt' er genug. Aber Buben
einen nur, und nur den dritten.
Da gefiel es dem Tischler — möglich,
daß er sich um die Arbeit an einem
zunftgerechten Sarge geprellt sah —, aus
Kistenbrettern ein Kreuz zu erstellen
für den Hügel aus Mehl. Das stand nun
plötzlich im Winkel und sagte:
Der Tod sticht über die Liebe.

V
Dead men are always right. You can talk
an hour along one line, and at last
you think you have everything proved, —
then they begin again with their silence.
Everything
you have said is refuted.

Benjamin kept silence in the wide chamber of echoes.
Modestly, but stubborn, not to be disregarded,
he waited, just as so often,
when the court convenes
a witness sits in the box.
Inside, in the hall, the tongues are flaming.
The robes hang like borrowed banners
about the starched collars of jurisprudence.
Plaintiffs, defendants play their game. Each
has his trump cards and draws upon them.
But then ultimately
the witness, the last one, is called. He steps
gently hesitant into the hall, — now
the defendant throws down the deck and gives up...

Countless times
Master Sergeant Wenig
had picked up his cards. High cards
he had enough but only one Jack
and that Jack-of-Hearts.
Now the carpenter, he took a notion —
perhaps half afraid to be beaten
out of a workmanlike coffin — to make
out of some box-boards: a cross to erect
for the hillock of flour. It stood now, the cross
suddenly there in the corner and said:
Death out-trumps Love.

Wenig wußte es gut. Doch immer
hatte er auf Vergessen gehofft. Nun war die
Karte gezogen. Es schien, als hielte
Benjamin sie hoch in der Hand. Und siehe:
Wieder nahten die Schatten, doch nicht mehr
jammernd wie sonst oder flüchtend, als sei'n sie
wirklich ein wenig in Schuld und bäten um Gnade.
(Herzbube stach dann immer: die Frau und die Kinder.)
Diesmal kamen sie schweigend. Sie schienen
gradenwegs aus der riesigen Grube gestiegen,
vorne den Ausschuß am Hals:
hier und dort ein paar Männer, meist Greise;
dann aber, ohne Ende, Weiber; Weiber und Kinder.
Ältliche, ausgelaugte, der Stammutter Eva
kaum noch verwandt, viel eher dem Weibe
Lots vergleichbar, nachdem es erstarrt war.
Und junge — häßlich und schön, mit Brüsten,
schwellend von Milch und Verführung, denen
Kinder anhingen: die Muttertiere
jüdischen Stammes mit ihren Lämmern.

Wollten sie es denn nicht wissen,
daß Jener nicht er war? Hatten sie nicht
gewittert, daß hinter der starren,
unerbittlichen Miene des Exekutierenden
sich der Andere verbarg: der junge,
unbescholtene Verkehrspolizist mit den weißen
Handschuhn, der täglich am gleichen
Platz, auf erhöhtem Podest,
sein Puppenspiel spielte, winkend und weisend
und manchmal
das brodelnde Meer verhaltend, damit ein paar Kinder
sicheren Fußes die plötzliche Furt überquerten,
oder daß er den nahezu blinden Amtmann
selbst hinübergeleite ans andere Ufer?

This Wenig knew well. And yet
he had hoped to forget. But the card now
had been drawn. It seemed it was held
high in Benjamin's hand. And look:
Shadows approached again, but no longer
moaning as once or fleeing, as though they
really were guilty a bit and begged pardon.
(Jack-of-Hearts had always taken the trick: the wife and the
[children.)
This time they came silently. They appeared
to have climbed up straightways from the gigantic pit,
with a bullet hole in their throats:
here and there a few men, mostly old ones;
but then endlessly, women; women and children.
Older still, worn out, scarceley kin any more
to ancestress Eve, but rather related
to Lot's wife, after her harsh transformation.
And young ones — ugly and fair, with breasts
swelling with milk and seduction, to these
children were clinging: the mother animals
of the Jewish tribe with their lambs.

Couldn't they understand though
that This was not he? Had they not
sensed that, back of the stiff and
inexorable mask of the Executioner,
the Other stood hidden: the youthful, the blameless
traffic policeman with the white gloves
who daily at the same post
on the high pedestal
played puppet games, beckoning, waving
and sometimes
holding the broiling sea back, so that a few children
might safely wend their way through that sudden ford
or that he himself might safely conduct the old,
almost blind judge to the opposite shore?

Dieser und jener war einer, war Wenig.
Innen und Außen. Man brauchte
nur die Schale zu brechen, da traf man den Kern:
würzig und mild. Verwirft man die Nüsse,
weil sie sich panzern?
War er nicht, auf dem Wege vom Bahnhof
(damals im zweiten Urlaub aus Rußland)
nahe daran, den Panzer zu sprengen,
als sie mit beiden Kindern neben ihm ging,
ihm, der gerade die dreihundert jüdischen Weiber
bei Saporoschje mit seinem Zuge
an die Erde verkauft, —
wie der Befehl es befahl? Büßte er nicht,
hier bei lebendigem Leibe mit Totem begraben,
was er in blindem Gehorsam im Lichte gefehlt?
Hatte ein Schwur nicht,
— unerbittlich, wie an der Pforte des Paradieses
mit gezücktem Schwerte der Engel —
ihm die Rückkehr verwiesen in das erbarmende
Mitleid, die menschliche Regung?
Ach, an das Jüngste Gericht
möchte man glauben: daß einstens,
wenn sich die Welt überlebt, Posaunen
oder Sirenen die Stunde verkünden, ferne
in fernerer Zeit... Es muß wohl
einmal alles nach einem Gesetz, nach
einem Maße gemessen werden. Einmal —
aber nicht heute, da jeder,
der uns befiehlt,
seine Gebote erläßt und jeden,
der sie mißachtet, verurteilt...
Aber Benjamins Schweigen
widerlegte die Ausflucht. Es sagte dagegen:
Schulterstücke und Eiserne Kreuze
kann man zwar von diesen erhoffen. Aber:
der die Krone ewigen Lebens verheißt,
hat das ältere Amt. Und zwei Herren
kann man nicht dienen.

This one and that one were one, they were Wenig.
Inside and outside. One only needed
to crack the shell and there was the kernel:
Spicy and mild. Do you throw nuts away
because they are armored?
Was it not he, on the way from the station
(during his second furlough from Russia)
who had been on the point of bursting that armor,
when She with two children was walking beside him, —
him, the man who near Saporoschje
with this platoon had just sold to the earth
three-hundred Jewish women, —
as the command had commanded? Was he not atoning,
buried alive here with dead things around him,
for the wrongs he had done in blind light of obedience?
Had not an oath,
— implacable, as at the Paradise gate,
the angel with unsheathed sword —
refused him return, into merciful Pity,
this human emotion?

Oh, the Last Judgement
one would like to believe: that the day will come
when World outlives World, when trumpets
or sirens proclaim the distant hour,
in a more distant time... Sometime, presumably,
according to one law, all must be measured
all by one measure: that day to come —
but not today, not when everyone
who commands over us,
issues his orders, and whosoever
dares disregard them is judged and condemned...
But Benjamin's silence
refuted excuses. On the contrary, saying:
Epaulettes and iron crosses
one can expect, to be sure, from these people. But:
He who promises the Crown of eternal Life,
has seniority. And two masters
no man can serve.

Plötzlich sah Wenig
die eigene Frau und die beiden Söhne
zu den Schatten gesellt. Und hatte Gewißheit.
Keinem ist es erlaubt, das Leben
um die Zeche zu prellen. Und Wenig
hatte blutig gezecht. Und war er geladen, —
der Gastherr hatte das Weite gesucht; die Gäste
mußten die Rechnung begleichen. Herzbube
war — wer weiß schon wie lange —
gestochen, verworfen. Nichts mehr
blieb in der Hand.

Jedermann kannte daheim den Wachtmeister Wenig
als einen Mann, der pünktlich am Ersten
seine Schulden beglich. Hauswirt, Bäcker und Milchmann, —
keiner hatte zu klagen. Und diese Regel
schien ihm auch hier noch verbindlich, im Lande
Niemandsland, Schattenland, Totenland... ach,
wer benennt es.
Abends, als sie die düstere Mahlzeit genommen,
hob er an, leise von Saporoschje zu sprechen,
zählte, erzählend, die einzelnen Posten
noch einmal nach. Und dieser und jener
klaubte aus seinem Gedächtnis noch dies oder jenes,
das zu der allgemeinen Rechnung gehörte.
Zahlen — sagte da einer —
können wirs nicht. Da muß schon,
wie das zuweilen im Haushalt der Staaten geschieht,
einer, der Macht hat, das Ganze erlassen. Denn —
wo kämen wir hin... Doch Wenig meinte:
Das sei eines jeden ureigene Sache.

Dann ging er hin — die anderen legten sich schlafen —,
lud seine Dienstpistole und zahlte,
was ihm geblieben. Wenig wars, —
doch der ganze Wenig. Und mehr
hatte er nicht.

Suddenly Wenig saw
his wife and their two sons
joining the shadows. And he was sure.
No one is really allowed to cheat
Life out of paying the check. And Wenig
had drunk bloody and deep. Though invited, —
the host had made himself scarce; the guests
had to take care of the bill. Jack of Hearts
was — who knew how long since —
trumped and lost. Nothing more
remained in his hand.

Everybody at home knew Master Sergeant Wenig
as a man who paid his debts punctually
on the first of the month: to landlord and baker and milkman, —
none had a thing to complain of. And this rule
seemed even here binding to him, in the land of
Noman's Land, Shadowland, Deathland, — oh
who can give it a name.
In the evenings, after they'd eaten their gloomy meal,
he would begin, softly to speak of Saporoschje,
counting, recounting again, the lists and the figures
over and over again. And this man or that
would claw up this thing or that out of his memory,
all belonging to the general reckoning.
Count? — somebody had said —
We cannot count them. Instead,
as it happens at times in the households of nations,
someone who has the power
must remit the whole thing. For —
where would it get us?... But Wenig thought:
That is each man's inmost affair.

Then he went — the others lay down to sleeping —,
loaded his service revolver and paid
the balance outstanding. *Wenig* it was
and *"wenig"* means *little,* but the whole Wenig.
And more he had not.

VI

Denke:
Die Erde würde dir einmal
aus den Augen genommen, länger,
als sie der Schlaf dir entzieht, —
wie durchschlüg es die Brust dir beim Wiedersehen
eines blühenden Zweiges! Du hörtest
alle Stimmen des Frühlings, schmecktest
die Früchte des Sommers voraus, röchest
des Apfels herbstliches Duften. Alles,
was du erahnst und, eh es Empfindung geworden,
durch entliehenen Enthusiasmus erschreckst,
hätte dann Raumzeit, sich zu entfalten,
dränge in alle Poren, auf allen Bahnen
deines Blutes zum Herzen, ruhte dort,
wüchse und träte dann reifer zurück
in den Tag. Denn alles größer,
beseelter zu schaffen,
haben wir Sinne.

Was erst hätte, nun da es zum Herbst ging,
jenen ein Apfel gegolten! Wie hätten
sie den verschollnen, den kommenden
Frühling empfunden! Sie wußten,
daß sie verschüttet waren. (Wir
wissens noch nicht...) Ihr Auge
war der Sonne entfremdet, ihr Gaumen
frischer Speisen und Früchte entwöhnt.
Was sie atmeten, aßen und sahen,
war trübe, war welker als ein
wesendes Blatt, das Vergangenheit atmet.
Ihnen war das Vergangene Mumie geworden.
Eingesargt in Flaschen und Blech lag die Nahrung.
Eingesargt schien die Zeit. Mumien sie selber. —

VI

Imagine:
The earth is suddenly taken
out of your sight, longer
than sleep withdraws earth from you, —
how it would thrill through your heart if you saw
a blossoming branch again! You'd hear
all the known voices of spring, and taste
the summer's autumnal perfume. For all,
all things you ever had thought (before they were felt,
frightened away by borrowed enthusiasm)
would have time-space, time and space to unfold,
pressing to every pore, on all the paths
of your blood to your heart, would rest there, growing,
then come back richer and riper
to life. For we have powers
to make things
more soulful.

What wouldn't (now that the autumn was coming)
an apple have meant to them! How would they
have felt the lost and the coming spring!
That they were buried, they knew. (We
do not know it yet...) Their eyes
were strangers to sun, their gums
disused to fresh food and fruits.
What they breathed, ate and saw,
was sad, was more wilted than
withering leaf that breathes of the past.
For them all past things had turned to a mummy.
Coffined in bottles and tins lay their nourishment.
Coffined was Time. They were mummies themselves. —

Benjamin hatte Frieden gefunden, und Wenig
hatte zu Ende gerechnet. Das allein
schien sie von beiden zu unterscheiden:
friedlos zu sein und immer zu rechnen.
Aber zuweilen,
wenn die trostlos hindämmernden Tage
nicht mehr zu deuten waren, die Leere
übermächtig den Bunker ins Nichts ausdehnte,
kam dann einem ein Traum, tränkte,
wie ein Engel den zagenden Christus am Ölberg,
den Verlorengeglaubten mit Stärke,
nannte nicht Herkunft und Namen,
Ort nicht und Zeit; war weder
künftig, vergangen: Anderem Leben
schien es entlehnt und anderem Sterne.

Der Tischler
hatte so einen Traum: Er fand sich
selbst auf grünender Wiese in Kindesgestalt
zwischen den einfachen Blumen sitzen, mit kleinen
Händen Gräser raufend und Blättchen zupfend.
Lächelnd sah ers und trat dann freundlich
zu dem jüngeren Ich und sagte:
Komm, wir sehen die Welt! — Sie schritten
langsam über den Anger, der gar nicht
enden wollte. Schon faßte den Großen
Ungeduld; er suchte nach Bäumen und Häusern
den Horizont ab, — da rief der Kleine:
Sieh doch, dort ist die Welt! — entwand sich,
eilte mit hüpfenden Schritten zu einer
hoch aufstrebenden, seltsamen Blume,
brach sie mit Vorsicht und winkte.
Der Große kniete zum Kleinen und
sah die Blume genau. Es war
ein Löwenzahn in der Frucht.

Benjamin had found his peace, and Wenig
had finished his count. This and this only
seemed to distinguish the one from the other:
to be without peace and be ceaselessly counting.
But there were times
when the disconsolate twilight days
no more could be grasped, when emptiness
stretched out forever over the bunker,
came in a dream to them, drenching,
like an angel the Christ on the Mount of Olives,
with strength those who had believed themselves lost,
did not give origin, name or direction,
didn't name place or time; was neither
future nor past: out of another life
this thing seemed borrowed, from some other star.

The carpenter
had one of his dreams: He was
by himself as a child in a greening meadow
sitting between the meadow flowers, with little hands
pulling up handfuls of grass and plucking petals.
Smiling he watched and then walked smilingly up
to his younger self and he said:
Come, let us see the world! — They walked
slowly over the field, which seemed not
ever to end. Already the older man
was growing impatient; he searched the horizon
for houses and trees, — when the little self called:
Why, look, there is the world; — turned away
hurried hopping and skipping to a
rising, reaching strange tall flower
and plucked it with great care and beckoned.
The man knelt down to the little child and
looked at the flower closely. It was
a dandelion gone to seed.

Er nahm den Stengel, auf dem sich die weiße,
fedrige Krone wie selbst trug, ruhend,
aber doch auf dem Sprunge, die Zeugung
neuer Welten weiterzutragen. Er wollte
lächeln, aber des Kleinen ernsthafte Miene
wehrte flacher Belehrung. Zum Scheine
sah er das kleine Lichtall genauer, prüfte
das Gewebe der hauchzarten Fäden und Stäbchen,
Wunder schwebender Architektur, und —
war davon schon umgeben, war drinnen!
Tiefe, endlos, und Höhe, nicht zu ermessen,
schlugen um ihn den Kreis. Die Wiese
schien ein fliegender Teppich im Weltall.
Und Kuno, der Tischler,
ruhte auf ihm, wie der Herr auf der Wolke,
damals, am siebenten Tag...

Als er erwachte, hielt er die Augen
lange geschlossen. Unbeschreiblich
vom Lichte erfüllt, wollte ers halten
hinter den Lidern. Als die andern sich regten,
sagte er leise: Bleibt eine Weile noch liegen.
Und er erzählte den Traum.

Schweigend hörten sie zu. Dann fragte einer:
Hast du die Sonne gesehen? Wie war sie? —
Ach, ich habe versäumt — sagte der Tischler —,
darauf zu achten. Sicher schien sie.
Aber wer sieht denn, wenn es so hell ist,
noch nach der Sonne...—
Warst du zu Hause? — Ich habe keinen
meiner Leute gesehen. Die Wiese
könnte vor unserem Dorfe schon liegen.
Aber die Wiesen sind überall gleich. —
War da ein Wasser? — Nein, ich sah keines. —
Vögel — hörtest du Vögel singen? — Ach sicher
sangen da Vögel. Hätte ich darauf gehört...—

He took the stem, on which the white,
feathery crown held fast, at rest,
but yet on the point, of carrying farther
the reproduction of new worlds. He wanted,
smiling to blow it, but the boy's serious face
forbade simple instruction. He pretended
to look the closer at this little world, testing
the tissue of tender threadlets and stemlets,
miracle of hovering architecture, and —
suddenly was surrounded by it, was in it!
Endless depths and heights beyond measure
closed their circles about him. The meadow
was a mere flying carpet in the universe.
And Kuno, the carpenter,
reposed upon it, like the Lord on a cloud,
on the Seventh Day...

When he woke up, he kept his eyes
closed a long time. Indescribably
filled with light, he wanted to hold it
behind his eyelids. When the other stirred,
he said softly: Stay quiet a while.
And he told the dream.

They listened in silence. Then one of them asked:
Did you see the sun? What was it like? —
Oh, I forgot — answered the carpenter —,
to give it a thought. Of course it was shining.
But when it's so light, who'd even look
up at the sun?...—
Were you at home? — I didn't see
any of my people. Maybe the meadow
lay before our village, though.
But meadows are everywhere alike —
Was there some water there? — No, I saw none. —
Birds — did you hear birds sing? — Oh, sure,
birds were singing. If only I'd listened...—

Hattest du noch deinen Daumen? —
Ich glaube, daß ich ihn wiederhatte.
Ich habe nicht die Daumen gedreht,
sonst wüßt ichs genauer.

Manches fragten sie noch, wie Kinder. Es stritten
Sehnsucht und Spott miteinander. Doch heimlich
wandte das Herz sich zur Hoffnung. Wir sollten
schlafen, immer nur schlafen können, —
sagte der Schreiber. Wir holten im Traume
alles, was uns hier fehlt: Sonne, Wasser — und Weiber.
Was wir hier unten leben, gälte als Nacht uns,
die man durchwacht. Und den Tag,
den verträumt man.

Schlafen... (hörten sie einen). Ja, schlafen...
Aber zu anderem Ziele. Ihr kennt nicht
die Legende der jungen Männer von Ephesus...?
Von diesen Jünglingen,
ersten Christen, die, flüchtig,
von den Verfolgern in einer Höhle vermauert,
zwei Jahrhunderte schliefen und endlich,
aus dem Grabe befreit,
ungealtert die ältere Erde betraten; —
so sehr gefielen sie Gott.

Wir — gefallen dem Teufel,
wollte der Schreiber dagegen sagen.
Aber er hielt es zurück. Er sagte:
Das ist ein frommes Märchen. Man könnte
sicher daraus etwas lernen. Nehmen wirs hin
als Beispiel guter Geduld. —

So will jeder ein Zeichen. Es traue
keiner dem flüchtigen Stigma der Freude.
Wir wählen Heilige
nicht aus den Sänften des Glücks. Im Schatten
ernten die Büßer das Licht.

Did you still have your thumb?
I think I had it back again.
I didn't twiddle my thumbs, though,
or I'd know more exactly.

They asked a lot more, like children. In struggle
were longing and scorn then. But secretly
the heart turned to hoping. We ought to
sleep, just be able to sleep all the time, —
the clerk was saying. We could get in our dreams
all that we're lacking here: Sun, Water — and Women.
What we live down below here, would merely be night,
which we sit through. And the day
we could dream through.

Sleep... (someone was saying) sure, sleep...
But for another purpose. Don't you know
the legend of the young men of Ephesus..?
Of these young men,
these early Christians, who, fleeing
were walled in a cave by their persecutors,
slept for two centuries and at the end,
freed from their grave,
not a day older walked the old earth:
so much they pleased God.

We — please the devil,
the clerk was about to answer.
But he held it back. He said:
That is a pious tale. Surely
one could learn from it. Let us take it
as example of patience. —

Thus each wanted a sign. Let no one
trust the fleeting stigma of joy.
We chose our Saints
not from the easy-chairs of joy. In shadow
the penitents harvest the light.

VII

Zeit — was ist hier oben die Zeit?
„Gestern", sagst du und „Heute", „Am Soundsovielten".
Morgens scheppert der Wecker. Von da bis zum
hastigen Frühstück, zur Tram, zum Büro
hast du ein Stückchen „Zeit" zu verbrauchen.
Mittags die Frei-Zeit, auf eine Sodaflasche gefüllt.
(Die ersten Schlucke verspritzen beim Öffnen.)
Dann wieder Dienst-Zeit, Geschäfts-Zeit; acht,
neun oder zehn mit der Stoppuhr gemessene Stunden
„Zeit" — wie Zündhölzer rasch verbrennend,
sauber geordnet, gezählt: ein jeder
hat seine Zündholzschachtel.
Tagesschicht, Nachtschicht, Sonntagsschicht,
Sonderschicht, Opferschicht —
Schicht um Schicht wird sie abgetragen,
Stunde um Stunde verbrannt, die „Zeit",
unerschöpfliche Läger, versteint und gehoben,
daß du sie eilig verbrauchst, Feuer
unter den Kessel, in dem man dich gar kocht.

Das ist die Zeit, die dich hat. Und die andere,
die du gern hättest, versteckt sich,
flieht in die Wälder, hockt in verlassenen Stuben,
schläft in Bibliotheken. Ein greises Fräulein
spult sie im Altersheim auf. Ein Mönch hat
ganze Ballen gestapelt; ein Zuchthaus
ein Jahrtausend auf Vorrat; verschleuderts.
Zeit zu finden, braucht Zeit. Wer hat die
eine, daß er die andere fände? Zeit
kostet Geld. Zu vielen
kann man sie billiger kaufen. Institutionen
gibt es für Frei-Zeit. Verbände
sammeln die Zeit, wie man Abfall
sammelt. Man haspelt —

VII

Time — what is time up above?
"Yesterday", you say and "Today", — "on the such-and-such."
In the morning the alarm clock rattles. From then till the
hasty breakfast, the tram, the office
you have a little piece of "time" to use.
Noon brings free time, filled in a soda-pop bottle.
(The first swallows spilt as you opened it.)
Then again work-time, business-time; eight,
nine or ten measured-out-by-the-stop-watch hours
of "time" — like matches quickly burning,
neatly in order, counted: each one
has its little match-box.
Day-shift, night-shift, Sunday-shift
special shift, Volunteer-shift —
Shift after shift it is carried away,
layered hour after hour burned up: "time",
inexhaustible resources, petrified and raised,
for you to use quickly, for fire
under the kettle in which *you* are being cooked.

That is the time that has you. And the other,
that you would like to have, hides itself,
flees into the woods, squats in deserted rooms,
sleeps in libraries. A graying spinster
winds it on spools in the Old Folks Home. A monk
has balls and bales of it stacked; a workhouse
has a thousand years in stock; throws it away.
To find time, takes time. Who has the one kind
so that he can find the other? Time
costs money. In quantity
it can be purchased more cheaply. Institutions
exist for free time. Societies
gather up time, the way one gathers
garbage. One winds up —

wie eine Maus in der Mühle —
acht oder zehn oder zwölf Tage herunter.
Alles ist vorher gerichtet. Ein Mannequin
steht die Natur schon bereit und trägt ihre Reize:
die blauen Augen der Schweizer Seen, die tiefen
Dekolletés norwegischer Fjorde. Montmartre
zeigt den Busen entblößt; und Neapel
trällert ein lockeres Liedchen. Ein Schauspiel,
greller als Grand Guignol; billig;
Attrappe.

Nichts hat mehr Zeit. Freude
kann sich nicht sammeln,
Schmerz nicht verzehren.
Worte sind Schüsse;
Gefühle Affekte.
Die Zeit sagt
heutzutage Tick-Tack
und empfiehlt sich —
bis zum nächsten Tick-Tack
und so weiter...

Tick-Tack sagte auch unten die Zeit. Eintönig
wiederholte die letzte Uhr ihre Lüge.
(Fata-Morgana-Oase in der
Wüste saumloser Zeit.)
Längst war der Faden gerissen,
von dem sie, wie Theseus,
Rückkehr erhofften und Rettung aus dem
Labyrinthe der Nacht. Eine Weile
liefen die Rädchen noch fort; dann stockte
unwiderruflich das Werk, und schweigend
trat aus dem Schweigen die ZEIT.

Sie schliefen, als es geschah. Und, erwachend,
eilten sie einem Entflohenen nach. Wie Herzschlag

like a mouse in a mill —
eight or ten or twelve whole days.
All is arranged in advance. A mannequin
Nature prepared to bear all her charms;
the blue eyes of the Swiss lakes, the deep
decollettées of Norwegian fjords. Montmartre
displays a bare bosom, and Naples
warbles a gay little song. A spectacle
harsher than Grand Guignol; cheap;
a swindle.

Nothing has time any more. Joy
can not gather,
pain consume itself.
Words are shots;
feelings are passions.
Time says,
nowadays: tick-tock
and takes its leave —
till the next tick-tock
and so on...

Tick-tock is what time said down below. Monotonous
the last clock repeated time's lie.
(Fata-Morgana oasis in the
desert of endless time.)
Long since, the thread was torn
from which they, like Theseus,
hoped for return and rescue
from the labyrinth of night. A while
the little wheels ran on; then irrevocably
the clockwork stopped, and silently
out of the silence stepped TIME.

They were asleep when it happened. And, waking
they hurried after a fugitive. Like heart's beat,

war das Ticken der Uhr ihnen heilig erschienen.
Nun, da das Herz nicht mehr schlug, schätzten
sie die verlorene Frist. Einen Maßstab,
schwankend genug, schien die Kerze zu bieten.
Sie wägten den Schlaf und das Wachen
gegen einander ab. Sie zählten
fragliche Tage weiter, durchmaßen
rastlosen Schrittes die Bühne der Leiden.
(Vierzig Schritte, langsam hin und zurück,
wie der Sekundenzeiger der Uhr, galt eine Minute.)
Aber das alles
war doch wie Abschied nehmendes
Nebeneinherlaufen an fahrendem Zuge,
Winken und Nachschau und Denken:
Jetzt ist der Zug da und dort. Und womöglich...
Aber es ist nicht zu halten. Du
fühlst
den dürren Behelf, und auf einmal
bist du im Leeren. —

Ein lautloser Wirbel
faßte sie, zog sie hinab, kehrte
Nächte in Tage, den Tag in die Nacht. Und endlich
ließen sie ab und fügten sich drein.
So war denn dieses die Zeit:
Daß sie spürten, wie Nahrung verbrannte
drinnen im Leibe und wie der
tierische Moloch sein Opfer verlangte,
die Reste ausspie? Wie er,
satt und gelangweilt, Ruhe begehrte und,
schlafend, Gier aufstaute für künftige Mahlzeit?
Oder war sie die heimliche Spinnerin Norne,
die an Abermillionen Fäden den Daumen
hornig rieb, das Bart- und das Haupthaar
länger und länger zu zwirbeln, auf daß es
Brust und Schultern zottig bedeckte?

the clockwork's ticking had seemed to them sacred.
Now that the heart no longer beat, they estimated
the interval lost. A standard of sorts
seemed to be offered by the candles.
They measured sleep against waking,
waking and sleep. They kept on counting
doubtful days, crossing with
restless steps the scene of their sorrows.
(Forty steps, slowly back and forth,
like the second-hand of the clock, counted one minute.)
But all of this
was like the leave-taking running
alongside a train already in motion,
waving and watching and thinking:
Now the train is at such-and-such. And maybe...
But it is not to be stopped. You
feel
the stupid makeshift and suddenly
you are in emptiness. —

A soundless whirl
seized them, drew them down, turning
nights into days, day into night. And finally
they let go and submitted to it.
Is this what time had become:
That they felt how nourishment was consumed
inside their bodies and how the
beastly Moloch demanded its victims,
spewing out the remains? How he,
bored and full, desired rest and,
sleeping, stored up greed for future mealtimes?
Or was it the secret spinster, the Norn,
who on millions of threads was rubbing
her thumb horny in order to twirl
beard-hair and head-hair longer and longer till
it shaggily covered chest and shoulders?

War sie das Wachsen der Nägel an Füßen und Händen?
Ging sie im Krebsgang und zog in den
unbarmherzigen Scheren die viere
in die Vorzeit zurück?

Sie wuchsen stummer als Pflanzen,
aber ins Dunkle. Dem Wurm gleich
gingen sie hin durch den Staub,
und der Staub ging durch sie. Sie wußten
nichts von der fernen, erahnten Maserung,
dem Querschnitt des riesigen Zeitenbaumes,
an dessen Wurzeln sie hockten.

Oben
strebte der Stamm in die Krone.
Bittere Früchte, die Heilkraft selber,
streute sie aus. Sie galten freilich
vielen als taub. Denn Zeit schien den meisten:
Warten auf bessere Tage, auf sicheres Schema.
Zeit war: Vergessen wollen und recht behalten.
Zeit war: Strafe, neue Verirrung, war Flüchten
aus der ZEIT in die Zeit; war Narbe,
mühsam verhehlt und geschminkt.

Hier unten
war sie Wunde, die brannte,
täglich strömendes Blut, nicht stillbar.
Jeder Herzschlag ein müder Hammer
auf die alten Gesetzestafeln. ZEIT war
da-sein und wissen
um die schneidende Fessel und wissen,
daß sie nur tiefer schnitte; war Fallen,
endlos,
in die Schwerkraft des Schicksals.

Was it the growing of toenails and fingernails?
Did time go backwards like a crab, drawing,
in her pitiless scissor-claws, the four,
into past ages?

They grew more silent than plants,
but into the dark. Like the worm
they went through the dust
and the dust went through them. They knew
nothing of the distant, guessed-at veining,
the cross-sections of the giant time-tree,
at whose roots they were squatting.

Above:
the trunk reached toward its own crown.
Bitter fruits (the power of healing itself)
it scattered about. They were considered
by many as dead. For time seemed to most men:
Waiting for better days, for a more secure plan.
Time was: to want to forget and remain right.
Time was: punishment, new wrong-doing, was fleeing
out of TIME into time; it was scar-tissue,
concealed, painfully rouged over.

Here below:
it was the wound that burnt,
the daily streaming blood, not to be quieted.
Every heartbeat a tired hammer
upon the old Tablets of the Law. TIME was
being and knowing
the cutting fetter and knowing
that it cut all the deeper; it was a falling,
endlessly,
toward the force of gravity of fate.

VIII

Wir nennen es Winter. Und meinen damit:
Atemholen des Lebens, und über Verwesung
kühles Leinen des Schnees. Ostwind ums Haus,
Nüsse und Wein. Die Mette, den Christbaum.
Freude, aufs Eis geschrieben, Spuren im Schnee.
Und immer der Wechsel vom Kalten ins Warme.
Später die Feste mit Masken und tanzenden Paaren.
Föhn in den Adern. Und Krokus in schneenassen
Fäusten des jungen Frühlings.

Aber da unten...

Wie Meltau legte sich Kälte
auf ihr kümmerndes Dasein. Unbändiger Frost
hielt den Bunker umklammert. Er kühlte
Decke und Wände. Wie ein Geschützrohr die
bloßen Hände ansaugt, sog der Beton
alle Leibeswärme an sich. In Kristallen
schlug sich der dampfende Atem
nieder am Stein. Das Blut rann schwer durch die Adern.

In steife Decken gehüllt,
hockten und lagen sie da. Der Kognak
war wie das Bett einer Hure: er wärmte;
aber die Wärme war jäh und erkauft
mit dem Ekel verrauchter Begierde.
(Man nahm ihn wie bittre Arznei
oder wie Rauschgift.) Gleich glühender Lava
kroch die Kälte, der Notwehr spottend,
weiter und tiefer. Sie rangen verzweifelt
gegen den unerbittlichen Feind, begruben

VIII

We call it winter. And mean by that:
the breathing of life and, over decay,
the cool linen of the snow. East-wind about the house,
nuts and wine. Morning prayers and the Christmas-tree.
Joy, written on ice, tracks in the snow.
And ever the change from cold into warmth.
Later the feast days with masks and dancing pairs.
Spring winds in the blood. And crocus in snow-wet
fists of the young springtide.

But down below here...

Like mildew the cold overlay
their miserable existence. Boundless frost
held the bunker in its grip. It cooled
ceiling and walls. As a gun-barrel sucks
the bare hands, so the cement
sucked up all body-heat. In crystals
the steaming breath precipitated
down to the stone. The blood ran leaden through veins.

Wrapped in stiff blankets,
they squatted and lay there. Brandy
was like the bed of a whore; it warmed,
but the warmth was violent and bought
with the disgust of consumed desire.
(They took it like bitter medicine
or like poisonous dope.) Like glowing lava
the cold crept, scorning their defences,
farther and deeper. They wrestled desperately
against the implacable foe, buried

einer den andern im Mehl, wenn der Schlaf kam.
Sie liefen im Raume,
rascher als der gefangene Luchs an den Stäben
seines Käfigs, wider und wider;
schlugen die Arme. Sie glichen manchmal
Hampelmännern am Faden einer
grausamen Teufelin, erbeuteten Gnomen,
die Willkür zum Tanz peitscht.

Endlos
schien dieser Weg durch die doppelte Nacht.
(Frieren heißt Verdunkeln von innen.)
Das Leben war noch daumenbreit groß,
kaum wie die Zunge der Kerze, die einzig
von der Sage der Wärme noch flüsterte,
als endlich die Finger der Faust
lockerer wurden. Im Tage
sprossen vielleicht schon die ersten
Halme aus der getauten Erde, als unten
Wasser in spärlichen Tropfen
neu von der Decke herabrann, süßer
als Honig von ersten Blüten, begehrter
als ein Brunnen dem durstigen Wanderer.

Langsam, der Wendung nicht trauend,
wälzten sie den schrecklichen Alp
vom gefrorenen Herzen. Die Stirnen
fühlten den Wind von Gedanken. Und wieder
regte Hoffnung die Wurzeln und blühte —
Wunder der Armut! — inmitten der Wüste;
Hoffnung, zag und bescheiden, auf eine
gnädige Fügung des Schicksals, auf einen
heimlichen Plan der zeitlosen Mächte.

each other in flour when sleep came.
They ran in the room,
faster than the captive lynx past the bars
of his cage, back and forth,
beating their arms. They often were like
jack-in-the boxes on the string of a
cruel witch, gnomes under a spell,
whipped into an involuntary dance.

Endless
seemed this way through the doubled night.
(To freeze is to grow dark from within.)
Life was still a thumb's breadth thick,
barely the width of the candle-flame's tongue,
that alone whispered a saga of warmth,
when at last the fingers of the fist
loosened. That day
sprouted perhaps the very first
blades from the thawing earth, while below
water in sparse droplets
trickled down afresh from the ceiling, sweeter
than honey from the first blossoms, more precious
than a spring to the thirsty wanderer.

Slowly, not trusting the change,
they cast the terrible nightmare
from their frozen hearts. Their brows
felt the wind of thinking. And again
hope stirred its roots and blossomed —
o wonder of poverty! — in the midst of the desert:
hope, modest and waiting, for a
favorable juncture of fate, for a
secret plan of the timeless powers.

Christof nannte sie Gott. Und der war gewachsen
aus Isaaks gnädig erlassenem
und Christi gefordertem Opfer, geschrieben
mit dem Blute der Heiligen
in den Sand der Arenen und an die
Deckengewölbe der Dome,
dreifach Dreieiniger Gott:
der Vater
der Sohn
und — vom einen zum andern
das stete Gespräch in der Liebe —,
der Heilige Geist. Und in diesem Gotte
trafen Äonen zusammen. Ihn glauben
war: im Denken zu sein
über alle Vernunft, im Frieden
leben im blutigsten Streite, Heimat
wissen in Fremde und Tod.

Christof hatte vor seinem Bilde gekniet,
als Kind schon. Er hatte
seine Augen geweidet an diesem
Wohnen im Glorienschein. Durch die Augen
hatte er dann ihn eintreten lassen
in das weitere Herz. Demut und Einfalt
hatten ihm dort eine Stätte bereitet, erhoben
über die Wechselfälle der Zeit.

Nun hatte Gott, still, ohne Aufsehn,
Christof lebendig begraben. Aber er war
bei ihm, stündlich und täglich.
Anfangs wie ein gestrenger, zürnender Vater.
Schließlich brüderlich nahe: Christus,
gefangen, verlassen, begraben,
abgestiegen zur Hölle und
wieder auferstanden dann
von den Toten.

Christopher called it God. He had grown
out of Isaac's graciously granted and
Christ's demanded sacrifice, written
with the blood of the Saints
in the sands of arenas and the
vaulted ceilings of cathedrals,
the three-fold tri-une God:
the Father
the Son
and — from one to the other,
the constant speech of love, —
the Holy Ghost. And in this God
aeons were met together. To believe
Him was: to be in one's thinking
beyond and above all season, living
at peace in the bloodiest strife, at home
in strangeness and death.

Christopher had knelt before this picture
already as a child. He had
feasted his eyes on this
dwelling in glory. Through his eyes
he had then let it enter
into his wider heart. Simple humility
he prepared him a place there, lifted
above the changes and fortunes of time.

Now had God, silent and calmly,
buried Christopher whole. But he was
with him still, hourly, daily.
At first like a stern and wrathful Father.
Finally close as a brother: Christ,
captive, deserted, buried,
descended into Hell and
risen again
from the dead.

Auferstehung
hoffte auch Christof, Auferstehung
im Fleisch und zur Freude. Doch:
wenn er betete, — niemals vergaß er,
jenes Gebetes zu denken, das einer
vor ihm gesprochen: Aber nicht meiner,
Herr, Dein Wille geschehe.

Dies war sein Kelch, und er mußte ihn trinken:
Ein Leiden, heillos und nicht zu lindern,
befiel ihn, hielt ihn
auf kärglichem Lager. Wie Lähmung,
außen und innen, bannte der Dämon
tödlicher Krankheit gemach seine Glieder.
Gichtig schwollen zuerst seine Finger. Dann
steiften Arme und Beine sich in den Gelenken.
Die Wirbel schienen gerostet. Und reglos
sah er die andern sich regen in neuem
Drange zum Leben. Selbst Atmen
war ihm ein Schmerz.

Eh es die andern erfaßten, war er
schon vom Tode gezeichnet, einem schweigsam,
bedächtig wirkenden, der Hast verschmähte.
Sie hatten rasches Sterben viel gesehen,
und Tod war, wei ein Blitz,
in ihre Nacht gefahren.
Nun trieb er wie der Schaft
von einer Sonnenblume, die im Schatten wächst,
allmählich in die Höhe, trieb
ums braune Feld der Leidenskerne
den gelben Kranz der himmlischen Geduld,
indes die runde Mitte, langsam dunkelnd,
den schwarzen Tod gebar.
Sie sahens schaudernd und beklommen.
Aber dann

Resurrection
Christopher hoped for: Resurrection
of the flesh into joy. Yet
when he prayed, he never forgot
to remember that prayer, that One before him
had spoken: Not my will,
Lord, Thy will be done.

This was his cup and he had to drink it:
a suffering, cureless and not to be eased,
came over him, held him
on his miserable pallet. Paralysis,
outer and inner, the demon of deathly
illness gradually spread on his members.
Goutily first his fingers swelled. Then
arms and legs stiffened in all their joints.
The spine seemed to rust. And motionless
he saw the others astir in their new
impulse for life. Even breathing
was pain to him.

Before the others had grasped it, he was
marked by his death, a silently, thoughtfully
working death that scorned any hurry.
They had seen sudden dying aplenty
and death had, like lightning,
struck in their night.
Now he was growing like the shaft
of a sunflower growing somewhere in the shadow,
gradually higher, gradually pushing —
around the brown center of suffering's seeds —
the yellow crown of heavenly patience,
while the round center, gradually darkening,
gave birth to black death.
They saw it, shuddering and oppressed.
But then

erfaßte sie ein Staunen. Ach, wie war
es leicht — so schwer es schien —, den Tod
als Summe, Endergebnis anzusehen:
Hier stehts. Das gilt. Nun
find dich damit ab! — Doch dieses:
ihn wachsen sehn, die Wurzeln ahnen
(die an die eigenen reichen!),
Stund um Stunde
dabei zu sein, — es wollte scheinen,
als habe sie der Frosttod nur entlassen,
damit ein dumpf Geahntes still sich kläre
zu reinem Wissen; daß sie lernten:
der Tod will Reife und die Reife Tod.

Sie pflegten ihn mit allem, was sie hatten.
Sie sparten sich das Wasser, das sie tropfenweise
und mühvoll sammeln mußten,
vom Munde ab, die Lippen
des langsam Siechenden zu netzen, hielten
an seinem Schmerzenslager Wacht,
sie überboten sich an Findigkeit, durch kleine,
vermeinte Freuden Dunkel aufzuhellen,
das doch kein Dunkel war. Denn dieser Kranke,
daliegend wie ein Stein, schlug Licht aus ihnen,
belebte sie mit seinem Sterben.
Er konnte wenig sprechen. Aber was
er fühlte, dachte, stand
wohl lesbar in den Augen, diesen Augen,
die einen solchen Sog von Licht verrieten,
daß nun die Kerze, die am Lager brannte,
noch ärmer schien — wie aufgesogen
von einem unsichtbaren Scheinen, das
aus Christofs Seele brach.

astonishment seized them. Ah, how easy
it was — hard as it seemed —, to regard
death as the sum, the end-result:
Here it stands. It holds good. Now
make your peace with it! But this:
to watch it growing, to guess the roots —
(that reach up to one's own!), —
hour after hour
to be there, — it almost seemed
as if death by frost had but let them go,
that a dimly-felt something might clear and become
certain knowledge, that they might learn:
death wants ripeness and ripeness death.

They cared for him with all that they had.
They saved up water, gathered perforce
drop by drop, painfully,
denying their lips, in order to wet
the lips of the slowly dying one, keeping
watch by his final bed of pain,
outdoing each other through little inventions
to brighten with supposed joys his darkness
that was not a darkness. For this sick man,
lying there like a stone, struck light from them,
enlivened them by his dying.
He could speak very little. But what he
felt and thought: stood
to be read in his eyes, these eyes which revealed
such a suction and wake of light
that now the candle, alight by the pallet,
seemed all the poorer — as if suctioned away
by invisible shining that broke and shone
from Christopher's soul.

Was tat er denn, das sie so seltsam rührte?
Daß sie auf einmal, wie zum Fest geladen,
längst Unterlassenes nachzuholen suchten?
Sie stutzten sich mit schmerzend stumpfem Messer
verstrüpptes Haar. Der Tischler wusch sich
den Leib mit Kognak, und die beiden andern
tatens ihm nach. Es war, als fordere
der Tod ein Feierkleid von ihrer Armut.

Lautlos war dieser Tod. Es schien, als wolle
er nicht mehr rühren an Entbehrtes.
Der Kranke war so ausgezehrt, daß seine Zunge
kein Wort mehr heben konnte. Nur die Lippe
regte sich manchmal im Gebet. Er lebte
mit abgestorbenem Körper, schien es, fort.
Und als er auslosch, wußte keiner,
was da zu löschen war.

Sie brauchten eine Frist, das Wort zu wagen:
Jetzt ist er tot.
Und als sie's sprachen,
wars tonlos Klage wie um ein verwaistes Haus,
das wohlvertraute Stimmen einst belebt.
Ein guter Geist,
vielleicht ein reiner Fürsprech,
war gewichen. Sie zögerten,
ihn zu begraben. Denn nun war er doch
ganz ohne Schmerz;
ein reines Beispiel,
dem sie trauten.

Er war nicht schwerer als ein Kind,
als sie ihn endlich
auf ihre Art zu Grabe trugen. Und das Wort
vom Staub, zu dem wir wiederkehren (das
der tote Benjamin ihm einst entlockte), stand
noch einmal auf, als sie das Mehl

What did he do then that touched them so strangely,
that they on a sudden, as if called to a holiday,
tried to make up for long sins of omission?
They trimmed, with painfully dull razor-blades,
shaggy hair. The carpenter washed
all over with cognac and the two others
did as he'd done. It was, as if death were
demanding some festive dress from their poverty.

Soundless this death was. It seemed he was trying
not to brush, not to touch things once given up.
The sick man was so weak that his tongue
could not lift one word more. Only his lips
moved in prayer sometimes. He lived, so it seemed,
on and on with his body dead.
And when it went out, no one knew
what there was to extinguish.

They needed some time, to venture the words:
Now he is dead.
And as they were saying it,
there was monotone moan as in an orphaned house
familiar voices had once made live.
A good spirit,
perhaps a pure advocate,
had disappeared. They hesitated
to bury him. For now after all he
was quite without pain;
a perfect example
in whom they had trust.

He was no heavier than a child,
when they finally took him
(in their way) to the grave. The word about dust
to which we return (remember
dead Benjamin lured it once from him)
stood up again, when they took flour

auf seinen Leichnam rinnen ließen.
Doch es galt
vor diesem Toten anders.
Hinter diesem Staube
war Licht und ließ ihn funkeln.
Als er sich
gebettet hatte, sah das innre Auge
für eines Blickes Frist
den unverstellten Schein.

and let it run down over his body.
But things were different
before this dead man.
Behind this dust
there was light that made it sparkle.
When he had
bedded himself, the inner eye saw
for the space of a glance
the unmistakable radiance.

IX

Das Schöpfrad ließ die Eimer kreisen,
hob, Zug um Zug, in immer gleichem Takte
ein kleines Maß der dunklen Flut empor
und warf es hinter sich zurück.
Monotonie,
die Schächterin der Seelen,
verrichtete ihr Handwerk stumm.
Die Opfer blieben
in ihrer Macht.

Zwar hatten sie den Namen „Leben"
noch nicht verlernt. Die Kerze brannte.
Doch brannte sie zum Ende. Jede neue
war wie ein Vorgriff namenloser Armut
auf einen Vorrat, den sie nie erwürben...
Die Nahrung, die sich einst im Bunker
schier unerschöpflich aufgetürmt,
schmolz wie ein Eisberg. Ihre Sinne,
kaum noch geübt, verkümmerten: die Augen,
im ewigem Zwielicht, trübten sich;
und das Gehör war blasig, unscharf —
wie unter Wasser.
Kaum, daß der Gaumen noch
die Speisen unterschied.

Laß ab vom Bild des Stammes, des gestürzten —
der ankert noch, vielleicht, mit einer Wurzel
im Erdreich —; laß vom Bild des Wurmes,
den du mit deinem Spaten teiltest!
So zwischen Sein und Nichtsein
weißt du keinen Fluß; kein Floß,
das auf ihm treibt, in keiner Strömung;
und keine Mannschaft,
die mit solcher Konterbande
noch Hoffnung hätte, daß sie Land,
das feste Land erreichen würde...

IX
The mill-wheel let the buckets circle,
lifted, one by one, in even rhythm,
a little measure of the darkling tide
and threw it backwards.
Monotony,
the butcheress of souls,
silently did her bloody work.
The victims remained
in her power.

To be sure they had not yet unlearned
the name of "life". The candle burned.
But it was burning toward its end. Each new one
was like invasion of enormous poverty
upon a storehouse never to be acquired...
The food, that once here in this bunker
had towered inexhaustibly,
shrank like an ice-berg. Their five senses,
scarce still aware, withered away: their eyes,
in constant twilight, dimmed;
hearing grew blowsy and unsharp —
as under water.
Scarcely the palate knew
one food from the next.

Forget the image of the tree-trunk, fallen —
anchored a while perhaps with just one root
in earth still —; forget the image of the worm,
which, with your spade, you cut in two!
Thus between To-be and Not-to-be
you know no river; not a raft,
afloat between, in any kind of current;
and not a crew
who with such contraband
could hope, could ever hope
to reach firm shore...

Der Schreiber,
kaum nüchtern noch und wie im Halbschlaf
von Rausch zu Rausche schwankend,
war schon gezeichnet. Plötzlich schiens,
als habe ein Taifun ihn jäh gepackt
und schleudere ihn umher; als sei
im Innern seines Leibes eine Springflut
von Schmerzen aufgebrochen. Kurze Weile
verebbte sie. Dann kehrte sie zurück.
Er schrie sich heiser; bellte; röchelte.
Ein Ende ohne Gnade.
Ein Verenden.

Nun war der Tischler mit dem anderen allein.
(Der andre mit dem Tischler, sollt es heißen.)
Vier Tote wohnten nun im Raum. Das Mehl
lag wie ein Schleier zwischen ihnen,
den Lebenden, den Toten. Aber wer
besteht auf dieser Trennung, unterscheidet
die Wasser, die sich schon vermischen?

Und doch — die Kerze brannte. Ihre Flamme,
manchmal sich regend, war wie leises Ziehen,
kaum merklich, unter der reglosen Fläche
des Meeres Zeit. Wer lange in sie starrte,
der sah vielleicht Bewegung
und wurde mitbewegt.
Und als die Zeit kam, da nur noch ein Rest
von einem Reste darauf harrte,
sich vollends aufzulösen im Verzehr, —
wie war auf einmal diese Feuerzunge kostbar
und wie umlauscht! In allem Ungewissen
war dies gewiß: das stumme Dunkel,
das auf der Lauer lag
und siegen mußte, würde
sich auf sie stürzen und sie blenden;

The clerk,
scarce sober any more and half-asleep,
swaying from drunk to drunken hour,
was a marked man. It suddenly seemed
as though a typhoon abruptly seized him
and threw him about; as though
within his body there had broken open
a well-spring now of pain. A little while
it ebbed. But then it hurried back.
He screamed him hoarse; he barked and gurgled.
An end *sans* Grace,
An ending.

Now the carpenter was alone with the other.
(The other with the carpenter, it should be said.)
Four dead men dwelt the room. The flour
lay like a veil between
the living and the dead. But who
insists upon this separation, distinguishes
the waters, which already mix and mingle?

And still — the candle burned. Its flame,
oft stirring up, was like a gentle sign,
scarce seen, beneath the unstirred surfaces
of ocean-time. Whoever stared her down,
motion he saw perhaps
and so felt moved.
And when the time came that a mere remains
of a remainder still was waiting to
consume itself and be consumed in light, —
how dear this tongue of fire now became
and o how courted! In all uncertainty
this much was sure: the blunted dark,
that lay in wait
and had to triumph, would
plunge down and blind them;

schmerzlos vielleicht; doch eben:
blenden.

Dann war die Stunde da: Sie hockten beide,
wie Freunde an dem Sterbebett des Freundes,
vor diesem letzten Lichte. Doch die Augen,
die brechen würden, waren *ihre* Augen.
Vielleicht ging einmal noch der trübe Blick
rundum;
nicht um zu prüfen — denn was da
zu ordnen war, war längst geordnet —,
nein, um den Sinn noch einmal an dem Bilde
der Umwelt wahrzunehmen, diesen Sinn,
der mehr als andere wog, selbst hier, da wenig
von ihm zu wägen war. Doch hinter dem Geringen
versank zugleich das Viele, das da oben
auf sie zu warten schien: das Grün der Wiesen,
Land, Himmel, Wolken, Menschenangesicht,
das Spiel von Licht und Schatten...

Was ungezählte Male schon
in diesen ungenauen Jahren sich ereignet
und doch nur Sinnbild schien, nun war es ganz
Ereignis, einmalig, unwiederholbar:
Die Kerze brannte nieder.
Sie zuckte her und hin. Der Docht ertrank
im letzten Auseinanderfließen. Schwärze
begrub den leichten Rauch. Ein Ruch
verkohlten Dochts stieg in die Nasen,
schwand hin und war
verweht...

Nacht. Nichts als Nacht. Doch Nacht hat Augen
und Augenlider, schläft und atmet.
Du siehst sie atmen. Und die Knospen
der Lider werden aufgehn, und du siehst es
mit deinen Augen, wie sie fibern
von jungem Licht. Und deine fibern.

painless perhaps; yet simply:
blind.

And then the hour was there: They squatted both,
like friends beside the death-bed of a friend,
before this final light. And yet the eyes
that would grow sightless, were their own.
Perhaps once more the darkened glance
went round;
but not to test — (for what was there
was long since set in order) —; no,
but to let sense perceive once more
that small world's image: This same sense
that weighed more now, even here, than most,
now there was little left to weigh. And yet,
behind the little sank the much that up above
seemed to be waiting for them; green of meadows,
land, sky, clouds, human countenances,
the play of light and shadow...

What countless times already
had taken place in these uneven years
and still seemed only symbol, now became
complete event, unique and unrepeatable:
the candle was burning down.
It trembled back and forth. The wick was drowned
in final dissolution. Blackness now
buried the flimsy smoke. A smell
of carboned wick prickled their noses,
grew thin and was
blown past...

Night. Nothing but night. Yet night has eyes
and eyelids, sleeps and breathes.
You see night breathing. And the buds
of lids are opened and you see it with
your eyes, the way they fever in young light.
And your eyes fever.

Und Aug in Aug, wie Pole locken,
wird Licht euch einen. Denn *ihr*
habt ja Augen. Aber hier
ist jedes nichts als blind.

Die augenlose Stille fühlte sich
wie eine Frage an. Und war es nicht
wie Antwort, daß der Tischler da
die Hand ausstreckte und die Hand
des andern ihm entgegenkam? Daß sie
sich aneinander lehnten, wortlos, wie
nach schwerem Traum die Liebende
nach dem Geliebten tastet, Halt zu finden
und Wärmetrost? Vielleicht gab noch
versiegter Tränenquell
den letzten Tropfen... Aber sonst
war nur die Kreatur, die sich
zur andern wendete,
nichts suchend als die Bürgschaft
geteilten Loses: Sieh, wir leiden beide
gemeinsam. Laß uns diese Nacht,
die unabwendbar ist, so Hand in Hand
durchmessen. Wo wir straucheln,
soll einer nun den andern halten oder
ihn mit sich ziehen in den Sturz.

Dazwischen aber raunte
das todbeladene Blut wie selbstvergessen.
Solang ich fließe, wenn auch keine Sonne,
kein Schimmer Lichts mich trifft,
ist noch das Ende
des krausen Wegs nicht abzusehen,
dem ich entgegenwandre. Ob ich hoffe,
ob nicht, — ich werde unter Tage
durch Schrunden, Spalten und Geklüft
der dunklen Sohle weiter wandern mit der Kraft,
die jede Strömung hat. Ich habe
nur dieses als Gesetz. —

And eye in eye, as poles attract,
light will unite you. For together you
have eyes indeed. But here alone
each man is naught but blind.

The eyeless silence let itself be felt
like a great question. Was it not
like answer that the carpenter stretched out
his hand and that the other's hand
came toward him there? That both, that each
leaned on each other, wordless, as
after bad dreams at once the beloved one
gropes for her lover, seeking to have and hold
solace of warmth? Perhaps the dry
and drying well of tears would give
its final drop... Or else
it was one creature, turning
unto another creature, seeking
nothing beyond assurance of
shared destiny: See, we are suffering both
together. Let us take this night,
that cannot be averted, hand in hand,
measure it through. And where we stumble,
there one can hold the other up or else
can draw him with him to the plunge.

But in between was murmuring
death-laden blood forgetful of itself:
As long as I can flow, without the sun
and even though no gleam of light anoint,
the end's not yet
in sight upon the crooked turning way
toward which I wander. Though I hope and though
I hope no more, — I shall apart from day
wander through crevice, cavern and through cleft
of this dark mine and wander with the power
that every current has. I have alone
this thing as law. —

So ließ des Schöpfrad seine Eimer kreisen,
hob Tag und Nacht in immer gleichem Takte
ein Lot der dunklen Flut empor
und warf es hinter sich,
zurück in diesen Strom, der uns
verschlingt und trägt.

The mill-wheel thus its buckets circled round,
lifting day and night in even rhythm;
A load of the dark tide comes rising up
and is thrown backward,
back into this stream that swallows us
and bears us up.

X

Licht, das aus tausend Augen sieht! *Wir* haben
nur diese beiden, die — wie Fingerhüte —
ein Meer ausschöpfen möchten, das
unübersehbar, unauslotbar ist.
Am siebten Tage unserer Kreatur
trat, was wir Licht zu nennen pflegen,
in diese Fingerhüte; und seitdem
vermeinen wir zu sehn. Jedoch —
wir sehen nicht. Aus uns sieht Licht.
Und was wir scheiden
in Hell und Dunkel, ist noch nicht geschieden.
Hell bleibt das Helle, und der Blinde blind.

Der Tischler und der andere... — willst du wissen,
wer dieser „andere" ist, so folge
mir nach. Laß deinen Mantel, den Hut...
Geh, wie du bist. Du brauchst hier unten nichts
als deine alte Blindheit, diese Nacht,
durch die, vorübergehnd, in einer Träne
ein wenig Licht aufblinkt. Vor Zeiten hätte
vielleicht ein Engel unsere Hand gefaßt.
Wir haben sie verjagt, indem wir sie,
wie einen Wellensittich der Metaphysik,
in goldbronziertem Käfig hielten.
Sie sind fort. Geflohn.
Wir gehn allein. Wir sind allein.
Oh, wie sind wir allein...

Du mußt dich fallen lassen. Diese Schwärze,
die dich erwartet, ist das Trauerkleid
des Lichtes, und der Schoß, der Knochenschoß,
in den du dich, ein Lager suchend, bettest,
ist derselbe, dem du einst
entstiegen, wenn auch damals

X

Light that looks out of a thousand eyes! — *We* have
only these two, which — like thimbles —
might exhaust an entire sea, that is
limitless, unfathomable.
On the seventh day of our creation there entered
what we are accustomed to call light
into these thimbles; and since that time
we think we see. And yet —
we do not see. Light looks from us.
And what we separate
into light and dark, is not yet separated.
Light remains light and the blind stays blind.

The carpenter and the other... — if you want
to know who this "other" is, then follow me.
Leave your overcoat and hat...
Go as you are. Nothing you need down here
but your old blindness, this night
through which, just momentarily, in a teardrop
a little light flares up. In ages past
perhaps an angel would have grasped our hand.
We have chased them away by putting them,
like some striped parakeet of metaphysics,
in gold and gilded cages. They are gone.
Fled.
We walk alone. We are alone.
Oh, how alone we are...

You must let yourself fall. This blackness here
that now awaits you, is the mourning robe
of light and, too, the womb, the bony womb
in which, seeking a rest, you bed yourself:
it is the same from which you once
climbed out, even though those days

das Fleisch noch über ihm erblühte,
das dich so oft getäuscht. Und die Verzweiflung,
die wie ein Nest von Schlangen deine Brust
bewohnen möchte, laß herein! Nein, lade sie
und alles, was dir nachstellt, ein zu diesem Mahle
an deinem roten Herzen. Laß sie saugen,
bis auch da drinnen Schwärze ist und Kälte.
Sie *kann* nicht schwärzer sein und kälter
als diese Nacht der schattenlosen Schatten.

Sprich nicht mehr von dem „anderen". Der andere,
den ich dir vorenthielt, hat keinen Namen,
der dir zur Trennung dient. Er hat wie du
aus einer Brust getrunken, Wind geatmet,
verraten und geliebt mit einem Herzen.
Zwei Fingerhüte aus dem Meer des Lichtes,
verschütte sie! Und nimm an seiner Stelle
den Fluch der Nacht auf deine Seele.
Sei unter Larven wie der Wurm im Holze
des Zeitenbaums, an dem der Stunden-Specht
mit seinem Schnabel klopft.

Du *mußt* vergessen,
daß oben einer auf dich warten könnte,
und vergessen,
daß er vergessen hat, auf dich zu warten,
und vergessen,
daß du vergaßest, daß er dich vergessen.
So voll Tod,
lebendigem Tod, und so voll Nacht,
gesehener Nacht, wärst du, vielleicht,
ein Raum, in dem ein Schritt verhallte;
ein dunkler, atemloser Raum. — Wie eine Uhr

the flesh still blossomed over it,
deceiving you so often. And the despair,
that like a nest of snakes may dwell
your breast: o let it in! Invite it in —
and all that stalks you — in unto this feast
upon your red, red heart. — Let them suck,
until there's blackness in it: blackness, cold.
It *can* not be more black nor colder than
this night of shadowless shadows.

Speak no more of the "other". The other,
whom I kept from you, has no name
to serve you for separation. He has, like you,
drunk from a breast, breathed wind,
betrayed and loved with a heart.
Two thimblefuls out of a sea of light,
spill them! And take in light's place
the curse of night upon your soul.
Be among larvae like the worm in the wood
of the time-tree on which the woodpecker hourly
pecks with his beak.

You *must* forget
that up above someone might wait for you,
and forget
that he has forgotten to wait for you,
and forget
that you forgot that he had forgotten you.
Thus full of Death,
living Death, and thus full of Night,
visioned Night, you might be (perhaps)
a space in which a step might echo:
a dark and breathless space. — Like a clock

am Bette eines Toten tickt, klopft nun
nur noch der Muskel-Specht in deiner Brust.
Auch dies mußt du vergessen: daß er klopft.
Vergiß, vergiß...

Und hast du ganz vergessen, was du einst
zu wissen glaubtest, und bist nur
um einen Seufzer reicher als der Staub,
aus dem du wurdest, dann —
dann bist du wie der andere,
BIST DER ANDERE,
der mit dem Tischler durch den Staub hingeht.
Dann hockt ihr beide da, schon Geistverwandte
mit jenen vieren, die das Mehl
in der Gestalt erhielt, in der sie gingen. Und vielleicht
ist auch das Wort vergessen,
das sie immer wieder schrieben
mit schwarzer Kreide auf die schwarze Tafel, bis
er sinnlos schien, der Name:
Hoffnung.

Salz. Wüste. Nacht. Verlassenheit. Vergessen.
Und nur der Specht, der — kaum gehört —
noch klopft...
So klopfte einst der Regen auf dein Dach.
So klopft die Hacke auf das Straßenpflaster.
Du hast es erst vernommen, als es schwieg.
Wie taub erst mußt du sein, wenn nichts
mehr klopft... jungfräulich taub,
taub wie der Adam, der aus Staub erwacht
und der nach innen horcht, wo dieser Muskel-Specht
pocht, pocht und pocht.
So hörst du's pochen, ohne es zu hören.
Und hörst es doch. Es pocht. Ach, Ruf und Echo, —
wie könntest du's noch trennen... Oder wie
sollten die Sinne orten können, was nicht Ort,
nicht Zeit verrät? Da pocht, gewiß, nichts anderes

ticking at a dead man's bedside, there still knocks
the beak of the muscle bird within your breast.
Even this you must forget: even that he knocks.
Forget, forget...

And when you've quite forgotten, what you once
thought that you knew and only are
by one sigh richer than the dust
from which you came: then, — then —
you are like the other,
YOU ARE THE OTHER,
who with the carpenter walks through the dust.
Then you two squat there, already kindred spirits
with those four others, whom the flour's dust
took in the form in which they went. Perhaps
the word, too, is forgotten
that they wrote again and again
with black chalk on the blackboard till
it seemed senseless: the name
Hope.

Salt. Desert. Night. Abandonment. Oblivion.
And only the woodpecker, who — scarcely heard —
still taps...
This way the rain tapped once upon your roof.
This way your heels tapped on the city pavement.
You didn't start to hear it till it stopped.
How deaf must you seem then, when nothing more
taps... virginally deaf,
deaf as was Adam wakening from dust
and listening within, where the muscle bird
knocks, knocks and knocks.
This way you hear it knock yet hear it not.
And hear it still. It knocks. Oh, call and echo, —
how tell the two apart? Or how
can senses place what shows no place,
no time? There knocks, for sure, none else

als dieser dumpfe Hammer auf den Amboß
zermürbten Herzens. Und er pocht
mit letzter Kraft vielleicht.

Und doch: Es pocht. Es pocht. Dein Kopf
pocht Widerhall. Das Klopfen tropft
aufs Trommelfell, wie unverhofft
der Tropfen klopft auf trocknen Block.
Du horchst: — — — Es klopft.

— — — — — — — — — — —

Es klopft. Und deine Sinne stürzen
wie durch ein Schleusentor
dem dumpfen Ruf entgegen;
und in die Sinne —
trocknes Bett von Strömen —
stürzt Ahnen, Fühlen, Wissen,
stürzt das Blut
von tausend Vorfahrn,
Enkeln und Geschlechtern,
das todbeladene, hoffnungstrunkene,
füllt
ein abgesunkenes Meer
mit jungem Wasser.

Du sollst — gerettet sein...? Wie soll dein Herz
dies deuten können! Hat es nicht genug
an Dasein, Gegenwart zu tragen? Muß es nicht
den Schlag aushalten, der es nun durchhallt
wie Schritt von Schicksal! —
Aber dieser Schritt
ist nur der Bote, den du ferne
in einer Wolke Staubes nahen weißt.
Die Botschaft aber...? — Nun,
da Zeit aufsteht und Ort sich wieder fügt
und Hoffnung das Geröll von vagen Jahren
urplötzlich grün durchstößt, — nun halte

but this dull hammer on the anvil of
the down-crushed heart. And knocks perhaps
with final force.

And yet: It knocks. It knocks. Your head
knocks echo back. The knocking drops
on drum of ear, as (undreamt hope!)
the dropping knocks on dried-out blocks.
You hearken: — — — It knocks.

— — — — — — — — — — — —

It knocks. And all your senses rush
as through a sluice gate
toward the dull call;
and into the senses —
dry river-beds —
rushes surmise, feeling, knowing,
rushes the blood
of a thousand forbears,
grandsons and generations:
death-laden, drunk with hope
which fills
a sunken sea
with new water.

You shall — be rescued...? How is your heart
to fathom this! Has it not enough
to bear of presence and existence? Must it not
shoulder the blow that so rings through it now
like step and stride of destiny? —
Yet this step
is but the messenger you know afar
approaching in a cloud of dust.
The message, though...? Well, since
time once again stands up and place takes place
and hope comes pushing suddenly green through all
the gray drab gravel of the vague years, — hold

den joch-gewohnten Nacken hin, den Spruch
des Schicksals zu empfangen:

Du wirst aus Staubes Nacht noch einmal
ans Licht gerufen. Du und jener,
der mit dir aufsteht, die ihr schmalen Schein
mehr ahnt als seht, der durch die Bresche
hineinfällt in die Gruft, und die ihr tastet
wie blinde Tiere zu den Stimmen hin,
die euch nicht meinen, — ihr sollt nun
den Blick aushalten, unter dem die Erde
von Blühn zu Blühen taumelt, der in Schwärmen
erloschner Sternenwelt noch nach-glüht... Oh!
Glaubt nicht an Rettung, die *ihr* meintet! Denn
euch ist die Scheidemünze „Tag"
längst eingewechselt in den Schatz, vor dem
die Kronen Scheidemünzen sind. Dein Auge,
dies Nadelöhr, hat Tage einst gefädelt,
wie ein Kind, das dir ein Tuch bestickt,
ein zittrig Monogramm,
so Stich für Stich. Nun aber wartet
diesseits und jenseits deines Auges Licht,
nicht aufgeteilt in Gestern, Heut und Morgen, —
Meere zeitlosen Lichts. Das ganze Licht.
Das Licht.

Die anderen sehen —
die euch erschreckt anstarrn wie Gnome —
nur dieses Bündel Mensch, aus einer Lauge
gefischt, die Form und Mark zerfressen. Aber ihr
wißt nur das Licht — Licht, das da innen
aufbricht,
Stichflammen gleich, entzündet
an diesem All, das euch begegnet
in einem Blitz, der Tod und Leben
zusammenfaßt und überstrahlt und aufhebt. Licht,
das tödlich heißen müßte, wär es nicht
das Licht.

the yoke-accustomed neck out to receive
the verdict of your destiny:

You are called out once more from dust's grim night
into the light. You and that one
who rises with you, ye who more guess than see
the narrow gleam that through the narrow breach
falls in the crypt, ye who are groping like
blind animals to reach the voices there
that do not *mean* you, now you must
endure the glance, the flow beneath which earth
staggers from bloom to blooming, which in swarms
of darkened star-worlds glimmers after still... Oh!
do not believe in rescue as you think it! For
the small coin "Day" is long since changed for you
into the treasure which (if you compare)
makes the world's crowns into small coins. Your eye,
this needle eye, has threaded days and days
like a child, embroidering a cloth or towel,
a trembling monogram,
stitch after stitch. Now however wait
this-side and that-side of your eyes' light,
not sliced to yesterday, today, tomorrow, —
oceans of timeless light. Entire light.
The light.

The others see —
staring at you in fright as if at gnomes —
only this bundle man, fished out of lye,
the form and marrow eaten. But you two
know only light — the light, that there within
breaks open,
like licking flames, enkindled
against the All, that meets you
in lightning-blaze, in which both life and death
are gathered, glorified and raised. The light,
which would be deadly, were it not
the light.

Du fühlst den anderen stürzen. Ihn zersprengte,
zerriß der große Augen-Blick (der erste,
der dieses Wort verdient). Ihn zu beklagen,
ist Irrtum. Warum willst du hoffen,
zu überleben? —- Übersterben,
das ist das Wort. Am Licht genesen
die Halben, die den Halb-Gott lieben. Schlacken
sind deine Tage, da du ausglühst
bis ins Erkalten. Die Erwählten
verbrennen augenblicks.

*

So ist die neue Sage, die vom Staube,
die alte nur vom ewigen Licht. Wir zögern lange
— ein Leben lang —, in ihr zu lesen.
Da steht der Staub auf, stiebt und wirbelt nieder,
bedeckt den staubgeformten Adam, wirft ihn
zurück ins Nichts und läßt ihn ruhen.
Dann ruft das Licht, Geschlechter um Geschlecht,
die Ungebornen, die Verlorenen, daß sie zeugen
aus tausend schwarzen Stillen endlich
ein einziges helles Kind.

You feel the other fall. He burst apart,
he tore apart under the great eye's glance
(the first moment that deserved this name). But
to mourn for him is wrong. Why will you hope
to outlive? - - To outdie,
that is the word. *They* are healed by the light:
the half-ones, those who love the half-God. Slag
are all your days, the while your glow dies out
into a coldness. But the chosen
burn in a moment's glance.

*

Thus runs the new legend, the legend of dust;
only the old is of eternal light. Long
we wait — a life-long — to read in it.
Now the dust rises up, clouds and whirls down,
covers the dust-formed Adam, throws him
back into nothingness and lets him rest.
Then light calls, generation after generation,
the unborn, the lost that they beget
from thousand darkened silences at last
one single child of light.

www.ingramcontent.com/pod-product-compliance
Lightning Source LLC
Chambersburg PA
CBHW031319150426
43191CB00005B/267